"This stunning new literary work illuminates the importance of archival in sound, archival in art, and in life. It is necessary to place our compositions, our performances, and our exchanges on this musical journey inside the afrofuturist architecture of our own making. As Black women it is imperative that we continue to be explicit and bold in our truth telling, our love, and creation."

Camae Ayewa aka Moor Mother, Co-Founder of Black Quantum Futurism

"*The Mandorla Letters* contains all the luminosity and human consciousness necessary for gaining critical insight for navigating the current cultural landscapes. This exquisite and imaginative work–part testimony, part collective memory–is essential for a new survival work-song. Part cultural analysis and criticism, part memoir of younger years, and part visionary radical self-reflection on the possible, Professor Mitchell Gantt, as musician, composer, poet, and teacher, gives us a book that is truly revelatory."

Haki R. Madhubuti, *Black Men: Obsolete, Single, Dangerous?* and *Taught By Women: Poems as Resistance Language*

"Epistolary speculation as memoir; performance document as romance; theory of collaborative composition as extended koan; notebook of a return to native land as otherworldly exit visa–*The Mandorla Letters* is unfathomably rich in praise and mourning and morning and impossible arising in devoted grounding and emphatic sounding. Nicole Mitchell Gantt is an absolute and indispensable celebrant of those rites. She knows that we are vulnerable. She knows this is our strength. She renews our ancient learning. She singsigns pearls in the mouths of our young."

Fred Moten, *In the Break: The Aesthetics of the Black Radical Tradition*, Professor of Performance Studies and Comparative Literature at New York University

Publisher
Green Lantern Press
www.thegreenlantern.org

Editors
Fulla Abdul-Jabbar
Caroline Picard

Distributor
University of Minnesota Press
111 Third Avenue South, Suite 290
Minneapolis, MN 55401-2520
www.upress.umn.edu

Copyediting
Larry Blumenfeld
Irma Nuñez
Lauren Weinberg

Book Design
Kizzy Memani
Lauren Williams

Typefaces
Avara
Happy Times at the IKOB
Aktiv Grotesk
Alegreya Sans

Printer
Permanent Printing, China

ISBN 978-1-7373028-2-7

Edition
First Edition 900
© 2022 by Nicole Mitchell Gantt

THE MANDORLA LETTERS

for the hopeful

Nicole Mitchell Gantt

*An open source of seeds
for anyone, artist or otherwise,
to fuel imaginations
toward the co-creation of positive futures*

This book is dedicated to
my hubby soulmate
Calvin Bernard Gantt,
who departed Earth just as
this book was completed.

Our many conversations
about the need for a
paradigm shift was a central
influence on this writing.

I love you Calvin,
to Sirius and back.

Thank you for being a
bright light and an ultimate
companion on the path of life.

Thank you for showing
me true love.

ACKNOWL-EDGMENTS

Immense thanks to Caroline Picard and Fulla Abdul-Jabbar of Green Lantern Press, who asked me to write a short piece for their pamphlet series *On Civil Disobedience*. The result, over four years, is this book. Caroline and Fulla, thank you for all your mentorship and encouragement on this organically maiden voyage of *The Mandorla Letters*. Copyeditors Lauren Weinberg and Irma Nuñez, I'm grateful for your detailed attention, and for your willingness to work with my unconventional language style and form. Lauren Williams and Kizzy Memani, thank you for bringing clarity to my overlapping mosaic through your wondrous book design. Khari B, thank you for inspiring the direction of the linguistics of my Mandorlian-speak. Many thanks to my insightful friends and colleagues who read with razor sharp eyes and gave me essential feedback to expand my awareness and expression in the work, including JoVia Armstrong, Coco Elysses, Joshua Kun, Sharan Strange, Imani Uzuri, Larry Blumenfield, Fumi Okiji, and many more. Special thanks to Baba Haki R. Madhubuti of Third World Press for your critical eye and longstanding guidance.

To Black Earth Ensemble friends/musicians of *Mandorla Awakening II*–Tatsu Aoki, JoVia Armstrong, Renée Baker, Hélène Breschand, Hannes Buder, Jakob Nierenz, Tomeka Reid, Mazz Swift, Kojiro Umezaki, Alex Wing, and avery r. young–I am grateful for your openness in sharing your sunshine, friendship, and creative brilliance that led to manifesting the musical performances of this project, and ultimately, this book. Ulysses Jenkins, thank you for your mentorship, patience and luminous vision in your video art for *MA I* and *MA II*. Gratitude to choreographer/friend Dr. Sheron Ama Wray and video actors Justin Beans, Pamela Davis, Maketa Daniels,

Calvin Gantt, Jason Poullard, Diana Schoenfield, Krystal Pires Patch, and Felicia Stock for your excellent work in Jenkins's *MA II* video art. Big thanks to sister/friend Azaziah Hubert for your beautiful representation as mother Goddess in *MA II*.

Thank you to the *Mandorla Awakening I* creative team, including video artist Ulysses Jenkins, choreographer Lisa Naugle, lighting designer Karyn Lawrence, photographer Joel Wanek, and costume designer/childhood sister-friend Jeni Hayes-Presnall for lending your amazing talents and vision! Musicians and dancers of *MA I*—Blaire Brown, Valerie Chang, Christine Gerena, Calvin Gantt, Lisa Mezzacappa, Nicholas Maldonado, Jonathan and Jared Mattson, Boroka Nagy, Laura Ochikubo, Anna Okunev, Tomeka Reid, Bobby Rodriguez, Paul Sinclair and Shih Wei Wu—thank you for sprouting the Mandorla project into this world through your works! Najite Agindotan and Maia, actors of *MA I*, thank you for your loving mentorship and for bringing your powerful presence to the Sky Mandorlians.

To Yolanda Cursach and Peter Taub, thank you for believing in my work and for your generous support for the production of *MA II* and *Intergalactic Beings* at Chicago's Museum of Contemporary Art. Mathew Pukulski of FPE Records and sound engineer Caleb Willitz, thank you for transforming our live concert into a published recording. Many thanks to University of California Irvine's Claire Trevor School of the Arts, Xmpl Theater, music department chairs David Brodbeck and Stephen Tucker, and Deans Joe Lewis and Stephen Barker who fully supported my creative research. At University of Pittsburgh, thanks to Dean Kathy Blee, music department chairs Mathew Rosenblum and Adriana Helbig, and creative faculty colleagues Michael Heller, Aaron Johnson, and Dawn Lundy Martin for your roles in supporting my new arts adventure in Pittsburgh.

Thank you to the forest of Heartland Oasis Farms for embracing Calvin Bernard Gantt, myself, and our family, and for contributing your positive energy to this book. To my Earth-departed husband, Calvin, thank you for seeing me through this project from beginning to end, for your willingness to do anything at any time to support me, and for your ever enduring love and lessons. This project and book are the fruits of our melding. Michael Eugene Mitchell, thank you for sharpening my mind and encouraging my curiosity. Joan Beard Mitchell, thank you for passing down the legacy of creativity to me, and for embedding in me the belief that art can hold, heal, and move us. Humble thanks to the Creator for my life and path, which led to you (the reader) and me sharing this moment together.

Nicole Mitchell Gantt

What is Progress?

Nicole Mitchell Gantt

Dear hopeful n curious ones,

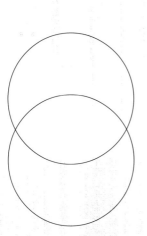

Sum of u r on erth, n some might b from other dimensions, having left erth long ago. May-b u joined this conversation from places I don't kno tha names of. We r all connected. We may each have a finger touchn tha one mind that intersects our core. N that non-physical space, when asking similar questions, perhaps we can all access related discoveries n insights. N Ma-land, we say there's nuthin new under erth's sun or any other. I just wanted u 2 kno that it's from here, tha mindlake, the maroon cloud, that we share this mandorla project stitched wi dream fragments intertwined wi tha nightmare challenges life has given us. Tha thread tyin it iz tha gift of breathing. Since erth iz a school, we wan 2 share our puzzle pieces wi yours, so we can all find our way thru this conundrum of suffering 2 tha happiness we all seek.

Liansee2

Map of Contents

v	Acknowledgments
1	Mandorla Island
4	Colliding Dystopic with Utopic Visions
22	Mandorla Awakening II: Emerging Worlds
28	What? A Mandorla?
30	A Celebration of Coexistence
40	We Are Vulnerable
46	western Faultlines
56	Our Invisible Thought-Agreement
58	Mind Decolonizers
64	Protest Music, Friendship Music
72	Together / Not Together
78	The Silos of Hierarchy
82	Unwrapping Positionalities
88	Right is of no sex. Truth is of no color.
90	Money Can't Buy Us Safety
98	A Visible Invisible
104	Gratitude
110	Listening Embrace: A Different Kind of Listening
118	Redefining whiteness
126	The Grit of Intercultural Collaboration
134	A Musical Village of Interdependence
146	What is Progress?
148	A New Life Paradigm
154	PROOF: The People's Right to Obtain Our Freedom
160	The Chalice and the Blade
162	Divine Motherforce
168	Dark Matters
174	Valuing Wisdom from Earth-Centered Societies
180	Messy Utopias

Letters

viii	Letter 0
38	Letter 1
42	Letter 2
114	Letter 3
132	Letter 4
166	Letter 5
172	Letter 6
178	Letter 7

Journals

26 | Entry 1

Emails

62 | March 20, 2018

70 | Entry 2

76 | November 16, 2018

Poems

97 | The Shiny Divider

100 | July 30, 2019

107 | Constellation Symphony

108 | Entry 3

122 | Staircase Struggle

131 | August 1, 2019

142 | Entry 4

144 | August 15, 2019

158 | Entry 5

186   Afrofuturist Visions and Octavia Butler
192   The Myth-Science of Humanity
194   Humans are Story-beings.

200   Banneker's Glimmer

206   Spirituality: An Octavia Butler–Inspired Earthseed

214   Letter 8

220   A "Seed" Springboard for Alternative Realities

226   Ideas to Support Human Happiness

234   Letter 9

238   The Dolphins and Swans Return to Venice

248   Undoing Race for a More Collaborative Game

254   March 22, 2100

Letters

185 September 5, 2019

198 November 19, 2019

204 March 13, 2020

212 March 30, 2020

217 Timewrap

218 April 7, 2020

222 April 30, 2020

232 Entry 6

242 A SCREAM

246 Entry 7

250 June 23, 2020

252 The Shiny Divider (Part 2)

Journals

Emails

Poems

MANDORLA ISLAND

In 2099, in the midst of the inevitable decay of World Union (WU) society, a vibrant, diverse, and technologically adept culture emerges on an obscure island in the Atlantic.

Mandorla Island is a richly fertile land of special Earth power and crystal waters that has remained hidden from the WU government due to the vibrational work of its inhabitants. Mandorla is an egalitarian society designed by people who have awakened their ability to communicate directly with the Source. Having survived the destructive forces of the Egoes Wars and the global virus, the Mandorlians have made a biological transformation after two generations of an Earth-centered lifestyle, making them permanently immune to the virus.

The story unfolds when a couple embarks on a journey outside the boundaries of WU and discovers Mandorla Island. Seeking amnesty in this foreign culture, the couple is astonished by the different life that Ma-land offers. Their own transformation beckons, even as they resist letting go of their old lifestyle. Shocked and inspired by the ways of the Mandorlians, the couple faces the reality that WU, their homeland, is coming to an end. When confronted with images of World Union shattering, the couple must choose to adapt to Mandorla or face death by struggling to help their old world survive.

"Mandorla Island," *Mandorla Awakening I*, 2013. Image by Ulysses Jenkins.

COLLIDING DYSTOPIC WITH UTOPIC VISIONS

Eeye: I've been with Uhuru long before she was born to be called *Nicole*, so I prefer to call her *Uhuru*, which is closer to her soul-name. We are most aligned when she dives with me into the *mindlake*. We are one. I'm her inner voice, her invisible backwoods part, and I talk through her, which is why we sound similar. You can call me *Eeye*, like the second *I* of Rasta *I* and *I*.

I've taken Uhuru to visit Ma-land many times, but when she wakes, she doesn't clearly recall. Fragments of her *mindlake* memory have mixed with her planetary reality to develop this project. You see, for Uhuru, the visions of award-winning science-fiction writer Octavia Butler seemed to intensify as she traveled deeper into the twenty-first century. Butler used science fiction as a vehicle to raise provocative questions about social inequities. Uhuru felt kinship with Octavia because her mother, Joan Beard Mitchell (JBM), was a self-taught Afrofuturist painter and novelist who expressed otherworldly visions in the '70s and early '80s before leaving Earth. Perhaps JBM and Butler had visited the same realms within the *mindlake* during that time. I know they do now. Both JBM and Butler, as well as Ben Okri and others, have recognized that human beings are still prisoners—we are in Part Two of the Abolition struggle to end slavery—at least to recent recollection. Slavery is much older than when people were forced to pick cotton and tobacco, but for your human short-term memory's sake, we'll stick with that. Just so you understand that Abolition hasn't been achieved yet.

This is mostly why JBM's dramatic suicide disturbed Uhuru as a teen: because Uhuru was so optimistic, she couldn't view JBM's departure as an escape from a dystopic prison. It seemed more like a wasteful abandonment, because of the blessings and utopic wonder of life. Uhuru decided to be an artist, like her mother had been, but she had the nature of playing with seemingly unsolvable problems like her engineering father, Mike Mitchell. Her father was anxious that the space people are so far ahead of us, and that we (the humans) were just not learning like we should, which caused him to always be in a hurry, going outwardly nowhere. So, throughout her childhood, Uhuru dreamed of space people visiting her and taking her around for fun conversations in an effort to solve problems. JBM had already written a map for space travel called *The Mind Shuttle*, but for many years, Uhuru was too traumatized by her mother's exit to use it. Uhuru didn't recognize that she was already a space being who was having a whirl at being human. Uhuru's mother seemed central to these interstellar visits, especially since they often dream-traveled in the *mindlake* together. Like JBM, Uhuru aspired to be the architect of artwork. That way the things she made didn't have to be absolutely correct and foolproof. Visionary art does not appear practical, but it can help us to fly. Uhuru intends to help us travel a bridge from the familiar into an unknown, just as JBM stood on a bridge between life and death when Uhuru was born and named Nicole.

As a young adult, Uhuru was nurtured in the Black metropolis of Shikaakwa (Chicago), on the southside full of caring faces, the place of her mother's roots. Shikaakwa, a stronghold for BAM (Black Arts Movement), was home to the self-determined artists who built Third World Press, AfriCOBRA, DuSable Museum, eta Creative Arts Foundation, the early rendition of Sun Ra's Myth Science Arkestra, the Association for the Advancement of Creative Musicians (AACM), and Congo Beach. It has continually transformed consciousness for generations and has long been a home to interstellar beings and expressions of liberation known as Black experimental art. In this culturally vast place, full of arts institutions and ambitiously creative peers, Uhuru found the primary support for her artistic and personal development for more than twenty years.

Books are doorways to other realms, and Uhuru had grown up mystified by JBM's esoteric library. Upon moving to Shikaakwa, Uhuru was drawn to Black books and became a cultural apprentice of Haki Madhubuti and Third World Press for almost 4,000 days. Haki Madhubuti is a publisher, professor, and institution builder. Uhuru also became a spiritual daughter-friend to the wisewoman vocalist and 20th century griot, Brenda Jones. Jones and her partner, Audi, would visit every now and then to stop time and to remind Uhuru of her original nature. She was repeatedly telling Uhuru that her flute could teleport, but Uhuru didn't believe her yet. Meanwhile, Uhuru sowed sound sculptures with the all-women's collective, Samana, where she learned aspects of Black womanhood that JBM hadn't had time to teach her, from multi-instrumental mothers Maia, Shanta, and Aquilla. Also, on another 4,000-day stint of the Shikaakwa period, Uhuru swam sonically in the Expanse and collaborated on the Dreamtime Records freedom ship with saxophonist and co-navigator David Boykin. After joining the AACM and soaking up much inspiration from improvisational soundscapes with soul siblings Hamid Drake and Glenda Zahra Baker, Uhuru formed the Black Earth Ensemble.

In 2005, Uhuru met Octavia Butler at the Gwendolyn Brooks Black Writers' Conference at Chicago State University, founded by Madhubuti. Immediately after meeting Butler, Uhuru was inspired to make music directly informed by Butler's *Xenogenesis* trilogy, including *Xenogenesis Suite: A Tribute to Octavia Butler* (FH12, 2007) and *Intergalactic Beings* (FPE, 2010). *Xenogenesis* expanded Uhuru's musical practice and, as no surprise to her interstellar background, she discovered science fiction to be an ideal home skillet for cooking up her visions of alternative worlds.

Not long after completing *Xenogenesis Suite*, Uhuru dove into the *mindlake*, and came back asking some questions that would lead her to the Mandorla project. I know this because I was with her. She asked:

What if we explored a conceptual merging of two opposing worlds: one dystopic and one utopic?

What does a society look like that is more egalitarian and has technological advancements that are cultivated in cooperation with nature?

Can an artistic performance incite us to imagine a transformation of human consciousness toward restoring balance between the Earth and people?

Can music catalyze a reawakening of human spirituality?

These questions compelled Uhuru to write her own speculative fiction to share with audiences through music: *Mandorla Awakening I* and *Mandorla Awakening II*, which is how we got here.

Initially, Uhuru imagined an artistic platform that could open doors to exploring how the ancient loss of feminine power to patriarchal rule came about, with the focus on a Goddess-inspired realm called Mamapolis. I had given her visions about all these Goddess artifacts in her meditations, and it made her wonder: How did souls in the body of women get to be so undervalued anyway? Uhuru wanted to find out. But, because American Earth had poisoned her perspective with the lifelong experience of racism, she wasn't satisfied that employing a gender lens on her project would help unlock the complex power relationships in society she was obsessed with understanding. In 2010, a new chapter of her journey brought her to Oneness-seeker Calvin Bernard Gantt, who showed her that shifting paradigms could change matter. Uhuru's mission in Shikaakwa was completed. Soon after, Uhuru's wordinizer soulmate, Calvin, gave her the confidence to share her story, not just through sound, but also through words.

She will continue the story as Nicole, but I will interject from time to time.

Nicole: In 2011, I left the nurturing, yet artistic pressure-cooker streets of Chicago and returned to the isolation-burbs of the Orange County (OC) of my youth to take on my first tenure-track professorship at University of California, Irvine. Upon arriving, nightmares of the violent hostility and racism I experienced in OC almost thirty years earlier flooded my memory. In the midst of Integration, my family had moved to Anaheim's clean sidewalks, where I experienced regular harassment by plaid-shirted men, angry over the arrival of a Black family who disrupted their precious vision of an all-white dixie-topia. The N-word practically became my name. A particularly enduring memory of being hated was when an older boy walked slowly up to me with a grimace, as if to give a half-hearted hello, but instead hocked hot mucus in my face and called me that word as he turned away, laughing. My pain was his pleasure. By 2011, OC was

"Mon, instructed by the Land Beings, appeals to the Sky Beings," *Mandorla Awakening I*, 2013. Performance still. Photo by Joel Wanek.

not nearly as "lily white" as it was when my family had arrived in '77, but a pervasive hostile vibe lingered.[1] In the 1920s, Anaheim had touted itself as a model city for members of the KKK and the John Birch Society (JBS), and by the '60s, thirty-eight chapters of JBS had been established there. However, in 2010, the Census revealed Orange County to be home to a healthy multicultural population. It identified "34% of residents as Hispanic and 18% Asian/Asian American," and yet, Black residents made up a staggeringly low 2% of the population.[2] This was the demographic on my return to OC. Even though 2011 was still early in the Obama era, which some had coined as "post-racial," several Black students from OC shared racial horror stories similar to my own. Meanwhile, at the very same Anaheim playground where I had been spat on more than thirty years earlier, my four-year-old grandchild was told, upon arrival, "I'm not playing with you. You're Blaaaaack." The child who uttered those violent words was not white. Racism was alive and well in OC, but now the initiators of anti-Black sentiments had expanded to include other People of Color.

In 2009, while I lived in Chicago, a narrative centered around a utopian realm, which I called Mandorla Island, had emerged from my mind. It was based on the question:

What does a technologically advanced, egalitarian society that's in tune with nature look like?

Then, in 2011, my frustrations with the stubborn pervasiveness of anti-Blackness and intercultural ignorance in Orange County informed my concept for the development of this seed idea into a multi-arts performance project, which began with a narrative and storyboard and grew into a social justice-inspired artistic collaboration. The 2013 premiere of *Mandorla Awakening I: Dorla Awakens* (*MA I*) was designed as an experiment in diversity, intended to exemplify positive relationships between distinctly different groups of people

---

1   Doug Irving, Peggy Lowe, and Ronald Campbell, "O.C. lost whites, gained Hispanics and Asians, census shows," *Orange County Register*, March 10, 2011, https://www.ocregister.com/2011/03/10/oc-lost-whites-gained-hispanics-and-asians-census-shows/.

2   "U.S. Census Bureau Quickfacts: Orange County California," https://www.census.gov/quickfacts/fact/table/orangecountycalifornia/POP060210.

(or beings) through the medium of artistic communication among dancers, musicians, and video-recorded actors.

"Dorla discovers new consciousness in an inner-stellar world."

I was seeking a bigger picture. Remembering a lifetime of being subject to cold hate and ambivalence based on my race, gender, or some other seemingly surface aspect of my being, I located the fresh confusion this caused me as a child. I wanted to understand the root of these power ruptures in society. Was it a combination of gender binaries, racial binaries, class binaries, and religious binaries? Throughout my explorations building this project, I became increasingly interested in base-hierarchical thinking as the root of human dystopia. Could I flip old hierarchies in this fictive, wordless drama enough to transform people's consciousness? My intent was to inspire alternative realities for how we, as people, relate to one another by redefining *difference*. A core idea of the project is my belief that:

Our imaginations can be keys to manifesting change.

Mandorla Awakening I used sound, color, movement, and video imagery to amplify how our actions and attitudes have a deep effect on the world around us. It explored life on Mandorla, a mythical place where the physical environment drastically responds to the attitudes and actions of its inhabitants: the Mandorlians. The different groups of beings who share Mandorla are more collaborative and interdependent than hierarchical. The project modeled a friendly coexistence, where I tried to exaggerate, in the extreme, how the actions of any one life-form heavily impact the experiences of all others. In *MA I*, video beings (Sky Mandorlians) mystically impact Mandorla Island and cooperate directly with dancers (Land Mandorlians) through silent gestures and spiritual energy to facilitate overall balance. Musicians (Land Mandorlians) have the power to impact Mandorla Island through sound. The story of *MA I* opens with the mysterious arrival of a human couple (Mon and Dorla) to Mandorla Island from the World Union through an ice cave. The couple is steeped in trauma

"Dorla arrives at Mandorla and communicates with Sky Beings," *Mandorla Awakening 1*, 2013. Performance still. Photo by Joel Wanek.

and illness, which immediately upsets the emotional and physical balance of the environment. This provokes the Land Mandorlians to initiate a healing ritual in collaboration with the Sky Mandorlians for their confused and sick guests.

Eeye: Uhuru doesn't acknowledge the spiritual content of this Mandorla project and others she creates. Through wordless interaction with movement, sound, and color, she was seeking to make soul connections with her collaborators and audiences. The telepathic interactions of beings from other realms expresses Uhuru's unconscious memory beyond being Nicole, beyond color, beyond race, beyond gender, beyond being human, beyond form. After all, some part of Uhuru recognizes that all life is connected and that she has not always been human, and neither has anybody else. Being on Earth is all just a wonderful experiment. If only Uhuru remembered this, she could probably be more holistic in her explanations, but it's my job to witness, not to correct.

Nicole: My involvement at UC Irvine as a core faculty member of the graduate program in Integrated Composition Improvisation and Technology (ICIT) was one of the positive aspects of my return to OC, along with living in the bike-, dog-, and café-loving, international/ multicultural little city of Long Beach, which was pleasant (as long as one could afford the Cali rent). To me, ICIT was a collective of musicians that happened to be college faculty; in our program, dreams came first, and the group could utilize the benefits of the university to realize them. Upon my arrival, we excitedly mapped out and grew ICIT from an MFA to a PhD program. Immediately, I was invited into research adventures with faculty trombonist Michael Dessen and bassist Mark Dresser, who sought to master the art of multilocational, internet-facilitated improvisational music performance (telematics) at UC San Diego. Faculty electroacoustic composer Chris Dobrian and I improvised with flute and electronics. I was also quickly initiated into Vice Chancellor Doug Haynes's diversity-focused Advisory Council on Campus Climate, Culture & Inclusion. The Chancellor's Office willingly supported my efforts to curate and present a number of annual events celebrating contemporary Black culture on campus, and supported my work as a new leader of the African American Student Experience (AASE)—a group of staff, students, and faculty members collaborating with Black student groups to improve the Black experience on campus. It was refreshing, after

A WORK IN PROGRESS

MANDORLA AWAKENING

FRI & SAT NOV 22-23, 8PM $15/$11
UCI's XMPL THEATER (CAC) BLDG 721

A MULTI-ARTS PROJECT

CONCEPT/MUSIC BY NICOLE MITCHELL
FEATURING: TOMEKA REID (CELLO)
BOBBY RODRIGUEZ (TRUMPET) SHIH-WEI "WILLIE" WU (TAIKO)
ANNA OKUNEV (VIOLIN) NICOLAS MALDONADO (TENOR SAX)
JONATHAN MATTSON (DRUMS) JARED MATTSON (GUITAR)
NICOLE MITCHELL (FLUTE/ELECTRONICS) PAUL SINCLAIR (CLAR
LISA MEZZACAPPA (BASS) LAURA OCHIKUBO (ALTO SAX)

VIDEO BY ULYSSES JENKINS
FEATURING: NAJITE AGINDOTAN & MAIA

CHOREOGRAPHY BY LISA NAUGLE
FEATURING: VALERIE CHANG, CARA SCREMENTI
CALVIN GANTT, BLAIR BROWN, STEVE ROSA
CHRISTINE GERENA, BOROKA NAGY

COSTUME DESIGN BY JENI PRESNALL
LIGHT DESIGN BY KARYN LAWRENCE

CTSA BOX OFFICE (949) 824-2747
CLAIRE TREVOR SCHOOL OF ARTS, UC IRVINE, 4000 MESA RD, IRVINE CA 92617

UC IRVINE | CLAIRE TREVOR SCHOOL of the ARTS
DEPARTMENT of MUSIC

Flyer, *Mandorla Awakening I*, 2013. Created by Nicole Mitchell.

ten years as an adjunct in Chicago, to be respected for my work and to find an academic community poised for collaboration, both within the Music Department and throughout the university. It was this support that made the *Mandorla Awakening* project possible.

Sunny UC Irvine has been heralded as a multicultural, federally designated institution serving a critical mass of Latinx, Asian, Pacific Islander,[3] and first-generation students, yet no US public university is offered a federal distinction (financial incentive) for increasing its inclusion and support of Black students. When I taught at UCI, from 2011 to 2019, Black students made up fewer than 3% of the thirty-thousand student population. Strikingly, this was the same percentage of Black students at UC San Diego when I was a student there almost thirty years before. Hence, as I intended to stir up stereotypes with my Mandorla project, I chose Black artist friends from Los Angeles (Najite Agindotan and Maia) to portray the Sky Mandorlians. Because of students' lack of exposure to Black culture and overexposure to racist ideas, I thought it would be fun to disrupt their racial biases by presenting them with what appeared to be Black godlike beings (Sky Mandorlians) presiding over the mostly white students playing the Land Mandorlians, and then to reveal how these different beings engaged in gentle, nonhierarchical collaboration. My husband, Calvin Gantt, who is a self-taught artist, played the main character, Mon, an older Black man cast away on an island of seemingly twenty-something-year-olds. Mon's partner, Dorla, was played by UCI grad student Valerie Chang, an Asian American self-taught dancer/actress. Both were purposely cast from outside the university's formal arts program: Mon and Dorla, the World Union earthlings disorientated upon their arrival to a new realm.

In contrast to OC and its strange racist hostility, Los Angeles served as a cultural oasis. In LA, I reunited with the flute innovator James Newton, my longtime mentor-friend, while making transformative musical bonds with vocalist Dwight Trible, drummer Dexter Story, pianists Joshua White and Billy Childs, and beat visionary Ras G. The World Stage in Leimert Park, founded by drummer Billy Higgins and poet Kamau Daáood, paralled the family vibe of Fred Anderson's Velvet Lounge in Chicago. The swanky Blue Whale in Chinatown became my destination for jazz. At LeRoy Downs's "Just Jazz" program in the tiny, community-filled art gallery Mr. Music-

---

3   UCI Office of Inclusive Excellence, https://inclusion.uci.edu/aanapisi/, https://inclusion.uci.edu/hsi/.

head, one could encounter jazz luminaries touring from New York or elsewhere. LA is where I reconnected with Najite Agindotan, my first improvisational mentor. A drummer/composer, Agindotan is primarily responsible for cultivating the Nigerian tradition of Afrobeat in Los Angeles. When I was a student in San Diego in the mid-'80s, he included me in his Une Igede project, an African diasporic group of musicians who played his music throughout Southern California. Une Igede was where I intuitively started to develop my improvisational language, while making mentor-friends from Ghana, Nigeria, Liberia, and Cameroon. I was the only woman in Une Igede and at least fifteen to twenty years younger than the other musicians, but I was always respected as a little sister. Returning to SoCali also allowed me to reconnect with sister-friend Maia, a multi-instrumentalist and multidimensional artist who had been an important AACM mentor. Back in Chicago, Maia and I—along with Shanta Nurullah, and then Coco Elysses, Regina Perkins, and Aquilla Sadalla—had co-founded the AACM's first all-woman group, Samana, in 1991. Maia, only fifteen years my elder, had been like a mother to me, especially during my own transition into motherhood.

MA I: Dorla Awakens was a wordless vehicle for communication between live music, choreography, lighting, and video.

"A couple awakens in another environment. Perhaps it's a new planet, or perhaps it's another state of mind. Either way, transformation is inevitable."

Eeye: It was not happenstance that Uhuru's first two spiritually influential elders, Najite and Maia, took on the important roles of the Sky Mandorlians in the *Mandorla Awakening I* project. It was no accident that Uhuru had returned to Orange County just months before her father, Mike, began his transition to leave Earth. The land of OC had gifts for Uhuru to make up for her difficult earlier years. It was a complete cycle for Uhuru to return to JBM's deathplace and perform this unifying ritual of *Mandorla Awakening*. Of course, Uhuru thought it was just an art project, but it was also a symbolic

"The Sky Mandorlians (Najite Agindotan and Maia) facilitating healing on Mandorla Island," *Mandorla Awakening I*, 2013. Image by Ulysses Jenkins.

reunion of energies with the intent of healing racial and other superfi-
cial imbalances between humans. Even so, bringing Najite and Maia
together to perform loving gestures as Sky Beings, was a recalibration
of their deep history together.

Nicole: Working from my storyboard, music, and script, Lisa
Naugle and Ulysses Jenkins, faculty colleagues from UCI's Claire
Trevor School of the Arts, consulted closely with me to manifest
the dance and video aspects of the project. Professor Naugle, then
chair of the Dance Department, is a renowned choreographer,
working with both improvisation and telematics. Her experience
with the former helped in preparing dance students for the improvisational nature of my music, while her telematic experience aided
her understanding of the mirage I hoped to create: dance-beings and
prerecorded video-beings communicating, as if in real time. Ulysses
Jenkins' reputation preceded him. A professor of art and a trail-
blazer of Afrofuturist video, Jenkins was the first colleague I sought
out when I arrived on campus because of our resonating interests.
Jenkins patiently helped me to do my first director's work with actors
for the video shorts, which, inspired by my descriptions in the script,
he then translated into his compelling imagery. Karyn Lawrence, now
an award-winning designer, was at the time an MFA student at the
Claire Trevor School. Lawrence had the challenge of rushing in to create
MA I's lighting design after another artist cancelled at the last minute.
    Visual artist Jeni Hayes-Presnall, an OC childhood friend, cre-
ated the otherworldly costumes for the Land Mandorlians. Jeni and
I had spent many of our youthful hours drawing and writing poetry,
and she had been mentored by my mother before JBM's death.
After decades of no contact, we united again to create this work. Her
participation infused some of our childhood magic into *Mandorla
Awakening I*. Similar to my mother, Hayes-Presnall was an isolated
artist, living in an environment where few supported her talent. The
MA I project served to invigorate her artistic identity.

Eeye: Another spiritual synchronization with this project was for
Uhuru to reconnect with her red-headed friend Jeni. They had been
an odd pair of friends as children, because Jeni's parents did not
generally like Blacks, and their age gap (Nicole at thirteen, Jeni at
ten) was seemingly too wide. Yet they had a spiritual history beyond
those years, which brought them together repeatedly to create
intuitive art. It was this friendship with Jeni that catalyzed Uhuru's
journey into creating. The costume design for *MA I* would be Jeni's

last artistic accomplishment before soon discovering she had terminal cancer. I'll let Nicole take it from here. My voice is within hers, after all, and I'll be watching.

Nicole: My *MA I* score was realized by a mixture of UCI students and faculty, as well as special guests performing roles as musicians, dancers, and actors.

MANDORLA AWAKENING I: DORLA AWAKENS

Mandorla Awakening I program

The seed idea of Mandorla Awakening is "Dorla discovers new consciousness in an inner-stellar world." The piece expresses an amplification of how our actions and even attitudes have a deep effect on the world around us, while hopefully inspiring our ideas of creative possibilities / alternative realities and raising new questions about difference. Although Mandorla Awakening has no usage of words, it is based on Mitchell's fictional story and she has been excited to see how it translates through sound, color, movement, and video imagery.

The Mandorla Ensemble is a mixture of undergraduates, grad students, alumni (as listed on the front of the program), and also includes Chicago cellist and long time Mitchell collaborator Tomeka Reid, Bay Area bassist Lisa Mezzacappa, LA stalwart star trumpeter (and UCI faculty member) Bobby Rodriguez, LA jazz violinist Anna Okunev, and SoCali jazz / rock phenom "the Mattson2" (UCI alumni), with Jonathan Mattson on drumset and Jared Mattson on electric guitar, and Nicole Mitchell on the flute and electronics. LA Actor/musicians Najite Agindotan and Maia serve a special role as "Sky Mandorlians" in the piece.

Communicating wordlessly through video to the dancers on stage, they represent beings from another more-advanced dimension. The Mandorlian dancers are all graduate students at UCI (as listed on front of program), with the exception of wild card actor Calvin Gantt and Valerie Chang (UCI undergrad) who experience reality on the physical plane of Mandorla, a land with double suns.

⟨⟨⟨⟩ **Musicians:**

Bobby Rodriguez (trumpet); Tomeka Reid (cello); Lisa Mezzacappa (bass); Jonathan Mattson (drum set); Jared Mattson (guitar); Anna Okunev (violin); Nicholas Maldonado (tenor sax); Paul Sinclair (clarinet); Laura Ochikubo (alto sax); Shih Wei Wu (taiko); Nicole Mitchell (flute, electronics)

Principle dancers:

Valerie Chang (Dorla), Calvin Gantt (Mon)

Dancers:

Cara Scremeti, Blaire Brown, Steve Rosa, Christine Gerena, Boroka Nagy

"A couple awakens in another environment. Perhaps it's a new planet, or perhaps it's another state of mind. Either way, transformation is in-evitable."

— from Nicole Mitchell's text "Mandorla Awakening"

1. **Mandorla Dawn**	7. **The Healing**
2. **Dorla Awakens**	8. **Union**
3. **The Meeting**	9. **Violence of Fear**
4. **Elevation**	10-11. **Diss-topia / Liberation**
5. **Merging Minds**	12. **The Return**
6. **Mon**	

This piece is a work-in-progress collaboration between CTSA faculty Nicole Mitchell, Lisa Naugle and Ulysses Jenkins.

Ulysses Jenkins (video): Jenkins is an award-winning visual artist and videographer, renown for his afro-futurist and socially provocative work.

Nicole Mitchell (concept, composition) is a flutist / composer, recently initiated into the first inaugural class of Doris Duke Artists.

Lisa Naugle (choreography) is an international artist celebrated for her work in exploring telematics, motion-capture and modern improvisation through dance.

The project premiered at UC Irvine's xMPL black box theater on November 22-23, 2013.

MANDORLA AWAKENING II: EMERGING WORLDS

I've always loved to have a second try at things. After the *MA I: Dorla Awakens* project, I was thirsty to play around with this Mandorla Island idea again. I asked myself: in what other ways can I reimagine new doorways through the template of this story? In 2014, I designed a class with grad-student artists at UC Irvine and guided them to create their own version of *Mandorla Awakening* with film, choreography, and music. I also shared my *Mandorla Awakening* idea with performance curator Yolanda Cesta Cursach at the Museum of Contemporary Art (MCA) Chicago and was granted the opportunity to do a new production of the project. In May 2015, my music group, Black Earth Ensemble, premiered *Mandorla Awakening II: Emerging Worlds*, featuring video by Ulysses Jenkins, as part of the Association for the Advancement of Creative Musicians' 50th Anniversary celebrations. A live recording of the MCA-commissioned performance was released in 2017 on FPE Records (Chicago).

Nicole Mitchell Gantt

These *Mandorla Awakening I* and *II* projects are rooted in the desire to inspire us to enlist our imaginations toward the creation of alternative realities.

What does a technologically advanced egalitarian society that is in tune with nature look like?

What visions does this question catalyze within you? It is intended to be a positive seed to springboard unlimited possibilities, artistic and otherwise.

Many of us have been taught to believe that to be creative is a luxury that most struggling to survive don't have time for. Artists have often been catalysts to help people imagine alternative technological innovations and to experiment with new ways of being. Dreaming of new worlds can easily be looked down on as overly idealistic or naïve. Critical theorist José Esteban Muñoz, in his book *Cruising Utopia: The Then and There of Queer Futurity*, affirmed my initial hesitation in focusing on a utopian vision. He wrote: "Social theory that invokes the concept of utopia has always been vulnerable to the charges of naiveté, impracticality, or lack of rigor."[4] Yet Muñoz also clarified how essential eliciting hope is to the making of visionary work, and how essential visionary work is to the catalyzing of substantive change:

> An antiutopian might understand [themselves] as being critical in rejecting hope, but in the rush to denounce it, [they] would be missing the point that hope is spawned of a critical investment in utopia, which is nothing like naive but, instead, profoundly resistant to the stultifying temporal logic of a broken-down present.[5]

---

4 José Esteban Muñoz, *Cruising Utopia: The Then and There of Queer Futurity* (New York: New York University Press, 2009), 10.

5 Muñoz, *Cruising Utopia*, 12.

For so many of us, yes, our present is dystopic and broken down. How do we get to futures that we want to actually live in? As we lament, we find technology—computers, cell phones, digital interfaces, and apps—at the center of our daily activities. (We are so addicted to them all!) These new technological inventions consistently transform our world—advertised with promises that they will make our lives better, happier, and easier. It may seem that scientists, technologists, economists, and transnational corporations are the most powerful stakeholders in our futures. Technology seems poised to hold the future of human consciousness itself. However, I believe that we, (regular, everyday people), collectively own our futures. Large corporations, employing innovators for their gain, seem more organized in engaging our imaginations and enlisting the power of our collective human consciousness than we ourselves do. Their goals are to make *their* visions manifest, often for *their* financial gain. But how are we actively (individually and collectively) harnessing the power of our own imaginations?

The filmmaker, science-fiction writer, and scholar Ytasha Womack, when presenting at the Amsterdam Sonic Acts Festival in 2017, shared her experience of visiting a Chicago elementary school. In introducing the concept of Afrofuturism to a class of Black fifth graders, Ytasha asked them to imagine a world they wanted to live in. These children expressed that they couldn't imagine a future, because their world was so filled with violence, poverty, pain, and fear. Our children are literally our future, and their imaginations will determine the future of humanity. It is intensely critical that we nurture our children's minds with hope and that we empower our own minds with new possibilities. With *Mandorla Awakening II*, the idea of emerging worlds was a way to affirm the presence of a multiplicity of futures that are available to us, not just a singular one.

I believe that our imaginations are key to changing our lives. If more of us choose to be imagination practitioners, we can individually redesign our minds and collectively co-create our future.

Nicole Mitchell Gantt

Entry 1.

Hi, umm, hello? Anyone? Am I online? This is Dorla. I've witnessed so much now. I need to record this.

First, I have to tell you, Mon is sick. He was sick before we even got here. The fever. But now he's not even talking. His fever is so high. I'm scared. It seems like weeks he's sleeping. They say it's his healing process. I'm not sure where we are or how long we've been here. I was asleep at first too. When I woke up, I was here. Where? I don't know. The people here—they. They're blue! We are somehow outside World U. I just have to have faith that these people know what they are doing.

One of them, Kisoka, she—I think she's a her? She's young like us. She's been nice. We, umm, they're not quite like us. Huge eyes and they're really short. Like, miniature short. But some of their hair is thick and locked like mine. Most of their skin is dark, but in different shades. Not brown. It's like a bluish-red. They all wear white. And it seems like they sing when they talk! They say Mon'll be fine. I've witnessed so much already that I have to record this with whatever battery I have left, even though I have no way to send it. No wi-fi here. They told me our love somehow brought us here? Are we dreaming? I don't know what the F that means. It's weird. But kinda beautiful. None of them are sick here, not like at home. You know how our places in WU are mostly glass and metal? Here, it's super alive. The buildings are small, like in a village. I can't tell what they're made of. Clay? Did they actually grow these buildings? They seem...alive. Seems like everything is bubbling and moving. Like underwater, but not wet. And trees! There's so many trees here, like in the old days before all the bees died. I can breathe! So much better.

They say it's called Mandorla.
They call us New Imaginers. They
said we can call it "Ma-land."

No wi-fi. Every time I ask, they say: "We don't have Y-fry." SMH. It's frustrating that maybe they have no idea what the internet is, so I have no idea what's going on at home or how to get back. For now, I just have to wait. It seems like they make everything happen with their minds? They only sing to us, but they understand each other without making a sound. Transporting, cooking, growing food—I don't see any machines or tools except for decorations. I don't know how they communicate across distance. There're no phones, no cars, no buses, no trains, no planes. I've seen the people appear and vanish in the blink of an eye. Creepy. But they have been nice and tried to be helpful. They seem as confused as me about how we got here. Another thing. There're no mirrors either. I know I look a mess. And the food tastes, ugh, weird—electrical. But it goes down OK.

WHAT?
A
MANDORLA?

A *mandorla* is a symbol—an almond shape created by two merging circles. I chose this symbol for the *MA* project because I interpret the mandorla to be an ancient symbol of wholeness. While the image might be most often recognized as an aura (halo) in early Christian art, the shape itself is much older. It is a symbol of the feminine, described in Hindu art as the *yoni*, and symbolizes the fertility of the Great Mother. I resonate with the mandorla shape because I visually relate it to the concept of inclusion, or a shared space within the merging of two spheres. Rather than choosing one thing over an "other"—a *this-or-that* paradigm—we can overlap multiplicity, much like Tao. We can embrace the diverse assets that come from each side. Rather than flipping a coin to choose either heads or tails, we can enjoy the whole coin.

Nicole Mitchell Gantt

"Mandorla," Damon Locks, 2016.

A CELEBRATION OF CO-EXISTENCE

The idea of merging realities/dualities/worlds is at the root of *Mandorla Awakening II: Emerging Worlds* (*MA II*). I was curious. Could I envision a diverse, egalitarian utopian world in tune with nature to merge with our present dystopic world? How could I symbolically collide dualities using sound? I decided to create an environment for dialogues of contrasting musical languages represented by the musicians in the project. *MA II* is a living sonic experiment of people practicing a musical coexistence while celebrating cultural and gender diversity and exercising a collaborative (intrinsically less hierarchical) platform of improvisation.

I chose my flagship composition vehicle, Black Earth Ensemble (BEE), to manifest *MA II*. Founded in 1998 and based in Chicago, BEE is a musical celebration of contemporary African American culture. While BEE is a family of more than thirty musicians, the instrumentation and personnel are chosen specifically for each project. For *MA II*, I chose to embody gender balance/fluidity, to have strong representation of Black women, and to include a range of contrasting musical traditions. Each artist in *MA II* is a friend and an ambassador of an authentic musical language and life experience. As a result, the performance contains an eclectic instrumentation of cajón, cymbals, banjo, electric guitar, theremin, shakuhachi (Japanese wooden flute), oud, cello, shamisen (Japanese string instrument), violin, flute, bass, and taiko (Japanese drum). I'm thankful to BEE musicians for their contributions to *MA*; all invested time and creativity in this and other BEE ventures, while simultaneously leading their own projects as composers, artists, and ensemble leaders. Their musical talent and their vibes as people have been essential to *MA II*. Who these artists are, what is important to them, and how they navigate their lives contributes directly to the symbology of *overlapping wisdom* inherent in the purpose of the Mandorla project. In a sense, we have all been growing up together as friends, and I can't help but smile about that.

Both Tomeka Reid and JoVia Armstrong have been members of Black Earth Ensemble for more than twenty years. They've been my longest-running collaborators, having played with BEE since 1999 and 2000, respectively. Tomeka is an internationally acclaimed cellist and composer who was raised in the Washington, DC, area. She works on a multitude of collaborative projects, ranging from free improvisation to chamber jazz groups to large ensembles with intricately written compositions. Tomeka is obsessed with learning, whether it's mastering a new language, finding new approaches with her instrument, expanding her knowledge of health, or navigating geographies across the globe. In everything she does, Tomeka dives in with full commitment and excellence and goes to the fullest extent. She often tours throughout Europe with her jazz quartet and is the first woman member of the AACM's legendary Art Ensemble of Chicago. Over the past several years, she's developed the Chicago String Summit as a platform to bring attention to string player composers and improvisers. I especially admire her work to uplift under-recognized legends, including Akua Dixon and Abdul Wadud, in her writing. Renowned for her versatile skill set, Reid has created her own improvisational language while staying true to swing and bop. Plus, she can play wicked bass-line grooves on cello and make unique sounds that will bristle the little hairs on the back of your neck with her highly emotive expressionism. Reid plays both cello and banjo in *MA II*. She has been an essential part of almost every Black Earth

Ensemble and Black Earth Strings project, including *Afrika Rising*; *Hope, Future and Destiny*; *Renegades*; *Black Unstoppable, Xeno-genesis Suite*; *Intergalactic Beings*; *Mandorla Awakening II*, and *Liberation Narratives*. In 2015, Tomeka initiated the collective trio, Artifacts, with drummer Mike Reed and myself, to celebrate music by composers of the AACM. At the time of this writing, she was the Darius Milhaud Professor of Music at Mills College.

JoVia Armstrong, a badass drummer, percussionist, producer, and composer, is from the legacy of game-changing musicians who graduated from Detroit's Cass Tech High School. We can add her to the list including Geri Allen, Marion Hayden, Regina Carter, Donald Byrd, Ron Carter, Alice Coltrane, Kenny Burrell, Dorothy Ashby, and others. JoVia's goal as a rhythmicist is to "challenge the concept of time informed by [her]extensive studies of music around the world, which allow [her] to play straight and swing at the same time."[6] Armstrong developed a signature percussion setup for the *MA II* project, centering the cajón (Peruvian box drum) with congas, cymbals, cowbell, hi-hat, and other auxiliary percussion. In *MA II*, she flexes in her playing to cover a great range, from sensitivity alongside quiet acoustic instruments to forceful dystopic grooves with electric guitar. As a member of Black Earth, JoVia also recorded on *Afrika Rising* and *Liberation Narratives*, and is the percussionist for BEE's *Bama-ko*Chicago Sound System* project. Armstrong creates new worlds with her ensembles, Musique Noire and Eunoia Society, and has worked regularly with the Afro-pop group Les Nubians. A member of the AACM, her recent work combines her Detroit gospel and jazz sensibilities with Chicago house music and experimental electronics. JoVia is also an award-winning teaching artist, having spent many years in Chicago mentoring young talent (including Chance the Rapper and Noname) in beat-making, producing, and songwriting. At the time of this writing, Armstrong was the Recording Secretary of the AACM and was completing her PhD in Integrated Composition Improvisation and Technology at UC Irvine.

Raised in Washington, DC, Renée Baker is the most prolific artist I've ever met. As an improviser on viola and violin, she heats up any musical environment with excitement. Her passion for life shines through her sound on her instruments, and her humanism has compelled her to become one of Chicago's most influential advocates for expanding Black representation in classical music.

---

6   JoVia Armstrong, email message to author, March 11, 2021.

The Chicago Sinfonietta and the Joffrey Ballet established some of the most diverse orchestras in the US as a result of her work as their contractor for more than twenty years. Baker is also one of only a few women to establish and conduct her own orchestra, the Chicago Modern Orchestra Project (CMOP). Baker's talent smashes boundaries: she is an incredible visual artist, composer, conductor, poet, film score artist, experimental filmmaker, and curator. Any day, she can be found curating an international film festival, composing new music for film, presenting CMOP for a crowded audience, exhibiting her art simultaneously in numerous galleries, or rehearsing an orchestra for a television screening. With CMOP and as an orchestra contractor, she has guided the careers of many Chicago orchestral musicians over decades. CMOP sets the example of a 21st century orchestra, through its focus on featuring living composers of all backgrounds, and its wide-ranging skill-set to perform western classical, new music, and improvised music. Of her creative process, Baker, an AACM member, has said, "Where rules only ruled before, I could now [as a composer] apply, ruminate, discard, or keep anything that served the purpose of expressing myself through music and actually activating my own visions."[7] Baker's friendship and her resilient spirit of fearlessness, humor, generosity, and maverick creativity have contributed bright energy to the *MA II* project, and to my life. Baker joined BEE in 2004, and has also contributed her essential sound to *Renegades*, *Liberation Narratives*, and *Intergalactic Beings*.

Alex Wing, an extremely versatile guitarist, grew up in Brooklyn, where he had access to live concerts by jazz artists including Barry Harris, Geri Allen, Stefon Harris, and Tommy Flanagan. In high school, Wing soaked up musical wisdom in master classes with the likes of Ron Blake, Carl Allen, and Jack DeJohnette.[8] As a culturally (not religiously) focused Ashkenazi Jew,[9] Alex strives to learn more about society's injustices in an effort to undo the orientation of his privileged background. We met around 2004, when Wing became a regular participant of the free jazz jam sessions at Chicago's Café Mestizo, led by saxophonist David Boykin, drummer Mike Reed, bassist Karl E. H. Seigfreid, and me. Soon after, we played together as members of the David Boykin Expanse, and Alex also became a

7   Renée Baker, email message to author, March 11, 2021.

8   Alex Wing, email message to author, March 11, 2021.

9   Alex Wing, email message to author, March 11, 2021.

member of BEE. Wing also teaches music to youth in Chicago. *MA II* features Wing playing blues and experimental rock on guitar as well as performing on the oud and theremin. He embodies virtuosity while brilliantly combining playfulness with intense respect for the tradition of each instrument he wields. Alex also recorded guitar on *Who Is This Girl?* and *The Aaya Sensation*, two recordings that feature my daughter, Aaya, as a child vocalist and songwriter.

Bassist, filmmaker, and taiko master Tatsu Aoki has been revolutionary in his development of a taiko legacy in Chicago. As the founder of Asian Improv aRts Midwest, he has defied the strict traditionalism often found in American taiko by creating projects that invite collaboration with African American experimental musicians from AACM. On bass, Aoki has a strong history in Chicago jazz, having performed as a longtime collaborator with renowned AACM saxophonist and club owner Fred Anderson. I still remember meeting Tatsu sometime in 1998, outside Fred Anderson's Velvet Lounge during intermission on a night he was playing with Fred. We didn't start collaborating until many years later. Tatsu founded and operates a program that teaches taiko and Japanese culture to hundreds of children in Chicago. Aoki grew up in Japan and belonged to a Toyoakimoto artisan family, learning flute, taiko, and dancing as part of his immersion in the traditions of geisha. I appreciate Tatsu's bravery in creating from his own vision, even amid pushback from traditionalists of Japanese culture. For the *MA II* project, Tatsu contributes as a bassist, a master taiko artist, and a shamisen player. At the time of this writing, Tatsu was a professor of film at the School of the Art Institute of Chicago. His creative video work has often been featured in *MA II* performances.

I've long been inspired by poet, author, composer, performance artist, and vocalist avery r. young, whom I first met in 1990 on the Black Chicago underground poetry scene. young grew up in the Black gospel community and absorbed Chicago house music and the local jazz and hip-hop cultures as a teen, just as he was developing as a poet and performance artist. He always struck me as an incredible talent who gave 110% of his spirit to any performance. His brutal honesty has been known to bring audiences to tears. When I asked him how he defines his music he said: "I am not a musician. I am a poet who has a keen way of expressing what I hear in my head to a root group of musicians who listen very well." His group, de deacon board. will have you jumping! young has dubbed this musical style *sousefunk*, a combination of soul, funk, jazz, blues, and hip-hop composed of sounds that would be ideal for a hip-hop producer to sample.[10] He is a gifted teacher who has worked many years with Chicago teens and incarcerated men. Though we met when we were both just starting out as artists, *MA II* was our first opportunity to work together. Through spoken word and vocals, avery brought my poems to life with an urgency.

Shakuhachi player Kojiro Umezaki is a core member of Yo-Yo Ma's Grammy-winning Silk Road Ensemble. A master of the instrument's traditional technique, Umezaki is also a versatile performer in jazz and contemporary music settings. In addition, he composes electroacoustic works that combine electronics with instruments of world music traditions in highly unique ways. Working at the intersection of technology and music, Umezaki has developed apps and many technological systems that utilize music. While I was developing *Mandorla Awakening I* and *II*, Umezaki and I were ICIT faculty colleagues at UC Irvine. Working with him as faculty, I recognized his openness to collaboration and greatly admired his fully expressive playing and singing style on the shakuhachi. Bringing Ko into BEE for *MA II* to share his artistry on shakuhachi was an opportunity for us to develop a friendship and to connect as flutists.

Ulysses Jenkins, the acclaimed video artist, painter, musician, and muralist, was raised in Los Angeles. He describes himself as a "video griot," whose work is inspired by African traditions. Music and poetry are central to Jenkins's visual storytelling. He believes in using technology to build community and was involved with some of the first-known telematic (multilocational art via television/video) experiments. He has been both an inspiration and a mentor to me, having supported my very first experiences as a film director and screenwriter for *MA I: Dorla Awakens* and *MA II: Emerging Worlds*. Ulysses's video camera work and creative images were essential to realizing both projects. At the time of this writing, Jenkins, a professor of art at UC Irvine, was preparing for a retrospective of his work entitled "Ulysses Jenkins: Without Your Interpretation" at the Hammer Museum and the Institute for Contemporary Art at University of Pennsylvania.

Choreographer Sheron Ama Wray—also a professor at UC Irvine and my only Black woman faculty colleague across four departments at UCI's Claire Trevor School of the Arts—helped realize the dance and movement

---

10   avery r. young, email message to author, March 11, 2021.

aspects of Jenkins's video for the premiere of *MA II* at the MCA. Ama, greatly inspired by jazz music, developed a dance company called JazzXchange in 1992 to renew alliances between choreography, improvised dance, and jazz. Ama also initiated a program that brings UCI students to the University of Ghana to deepen their understanding of what she calls "Embodiology," her inspired approach to African dance.

Visual artist, poet, composer, and vocalist Damon Locks, with whom I collaborated over the years in Rob Mazurek's Exploding Star Orchestra (ESO), helped to crystallize the Mandorla symbology of my imaginings by designing the album artwork for *Mandorla Awakening II: Emerging Worlds*. Damon's artwork is also featured in the background of the Black Earth Ensemble photo for the project. I view Damon's visual work as powerfully linked to the legacy of graphic artist Emory Douglas, whose socially conscious art was central to the Black Panther Party. Musically, Damon has been a rock star with the Eternals with Wayne Montana, while making riveting poetry and spoken word for ESO. In 2015, Locks, Lisa E. Harris, and I were in residency at The New Quorum in New Orleans, and he shared with us that his sense of purpose with his art had deepened after spending significant time as an art teacher for incarcerated people. Perhaps the result is Damon's most recent project at the time of this writing, Black Monument Ensemble, which places Black women front and center in a choir of singers and dancers that stunningly emanate hope and love for the Black community with a sonic energy that can heal all of us.

While performing *MA II* in Chicago, New York, Amherst, Berlin, Paris, Stockholm, and Lisbon, BEE made many friends along the way who joined the project. Berlin-based Hannes Buder brought new, chameleon colors to the *Mandorla* role of electric guitar; New York-based Mazz Swift stunned us with her heroic violin; Lübeck-based cellist Jakob Nierenz brought new grooves to our "Listening Embrace"; and Paris-based harpist Hélène Breschand became an essential conduit to the magic of Mandorla Island.

With this collection of uniquely talented people, *Mandorla Awakening II* united diverse musical traditions within a concert setting, while also venturing into new experimental territory. The fruitfulness of my explorations with this project notwithstanding, I recognize the limitations of my vision. I realize that part of my decision to focus on Black and Asian collaboration in *MA II* was in direct response to the lack of positive examples of Black and Asian social relations available to me while living in SoCali. I wanted to create a model that highlighted and deepened understanding and resonance between these two groups. However, there are endless configurations that can model intercultural coexis-

Black Earth Ensemble, 2017 (*from left to right*: Tatsu Aoki, avery r. young, JoVia Armstrong, Kojiro Umezaki, Renée Baker, Alex Wing, Nicole Mitchell, and Tomeka Reid). Photo by Michael Jackson. Artwork by Damon Locks.

tence with gender balance. Creative musicians such as Don Cherry, Butch Morris, Hamid Drake, William Parker, Alice Coltrane, Archie Shepp, Mark Dresser, Adam Rudolph, Renée Baker, Tatsu Aoki, and many others have been exploring how musical languages can translate across cultures for countless decades. *MA I* and *II* are just two possible imaginings of the Mandorla Island concept and narrative. That's why I invite others to explore the *MA* concept to create their own possibilities for including and collaborating with musicians from varying traditions.

Nicole Mitchell Gantt

My children,

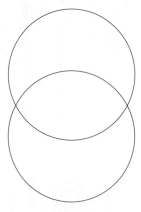

Teranthia will tell you, Ma-land came to b, cuz the mindlake. We stay woke n mindlake, while World Union sleeps. Tha mindlake is exhilaratn. Mindlake is where we have collective unity n connection 2 tha Sorce. Itz intoxican. Ah, itz our joy n jubulence!! Ma-landians love 2 talk bout mindlake sessions, n frequent. Itz most ahmazing 2 experience with partner, when both woke n mindlake! We see n talk to Ma-landian ancestors, relatives Liansee2 n Acorately there. They told us how they achieved duo mindfulness n mindlake. They was tha 1st dreamswimmas. Together they made Ephemera Island from blueseed in mindlake. Wow! To make a planet! That can only happen with real love. U need focus n melanin activated too. Liansee2 n Acorately was twin souls. They heard tha Sorce. Made new realm come alive, only 4 those redy. That is our blessing.

WE ARE VULNERABLE

Earth is rich with waters and soils, full of plants that provide the foundation for life. I like to refer to our planet as a plant-network; without plants, we and other life forms cannot exist. As vulnerable dependents on our planet, we can attain universal security (collective well-being), health, and happiness through embracing the idea of Oneness, not separation from others. My husband, Calvin Gantt, a writer, organic gardener, spoken-word artist, and interfaith minister, often talks of *Oneness* as key to increasing human well-being. He is concerned that society has increasingly encouraged separation, which disrupts communication and understanding between family members, close friends, neighbors, communities, and even countries. Calvin and I agree that human unification toward Oneness, toward communitarianism, toward embracing the other can be achieved

Nicole Mitchell Gantt

through awareness of our collective vulnerability, combined with respect for our individual diversity.

Much of popular music of the past several decades is LOUD, and sonically expresses strength, anger, and power. But our reality as humans is that we are fragile. We are dependent on Mama Earth to provide us with life. We are dependent on one another for community, safety, and happiness. We are vulnerable. In *Mandorla Awakening II*, it was important to sometimes conjure sonic vulnerability with naturally quiet instruments. Since amplified music came about more than eighty years ago, perhaps we've been conditioned to like most of our music LOUD. For the *MA II* 2015 premiere at the MCA in Chicago, BEE fluctuated between loud amplification and unamplified acoustic instruments. Quieter instruments such as Umezaki's shakuhachi, Aoki's shamisen, and Reid's banjo were mostly featured without amplification. Other instruments, including my flute, Baker's violin, young's vocals, and Reid's cello, had variable roles; they were sometimes amplified and sometimes acoustic, depending on the needs of the musical moment. This extreme contrast of dynamics was intended to express human vulnerability to the audience, and to compel listeners to lean in or pull back.

Nicole Mitchell Gantt

Chilren, yes.

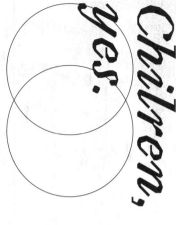

Teranthia say mindwrap sessions key to how we found blueseed n made our nu tech. Ah, bless, we connect once a day in mindwrap, 2 recenter our collective purpose w tha Sorce 2 do our vibrational work. Itz at dark b4 dawn when we dreamtravel (dreamswimmn). At that time, mindwrap is a quiet lake. Itz full n deep n clear. So beautiful. Itz surrounded w gentle rings expanding out n2 everyone's consciousness from tha Sorce. Everyone. Even those in WU. Not only does it sync up all of us w all beings, it also nips our illness at tha bud. Mindlake generates healing right at tha conception of illness. We learned that all that WU illness is so unnecessary. For all those thousands of years—what a waste! The key, tha root, waz negative mind thoughts. And screentime on those movies, tv, n computer n phones? Those just added 2 tha misery. Only screen u need is tha mind. Seen? Anxiety must b addressed immediately. That makes sure great health for us 2 prosper n. Thats why we must b careful w our visitors. They must feel comfort or their stress can destroy Ma-land. Dreamswimmas swim 2 mindlake depths. They excavate inventions from Sorce. The more Ma-landian collective clarity, tha more growth n it encourages our isle flourish. Im Teranthia, and yes, itz true, Ima dreamswimma. Most of us can only stay woke 2 seconds tha most in mindwrap, but those seconds made us able 2 achieve so very much. All that Mon and Dorla are witnessing now here was made from dreamswimmn. For dreamswimmas, itz a gift 2 have tha energy 2 focus inside mindwrap. I have not seen mindlake bottm but seen sides of red cliffs n entered knowledge cave. Ah, n Kishoka, my friend, found n touched blueseeds! Thats much talked about! Inside each blueseed is n entire nu universe. Each blueseed can offer up life anu. Each seed brings that chance, n each world with a slightly different ecosystem.

MANDORLA AWAKENING II

EMERGING WORLDS

" What would a truly egalitarian world
with advanced technology that is tune
with Nature look like?!!"

WHAT IS PROGRESS?

M1. EGOES WARS

M2. SUB-MISSION

M3. THE CHALICE

M4. DANCE OF MANY HANDS

M5. Listening EMBROCE

M6. Forestwoll Timewolk

M7. Staircose Struggle

M8. Shining Divider

M9. Mandorla Island

M10. Time WRAP

P2

Mandorla Awakening II, 2015. Playlist by Nicole Mitchell.

WESTERN FAULTLINES

My compositional process for *Mandorla Awakening II* was informed by my concern that the western world has hit a wall and must change. (I spell *western*, *white*, and *european* without caps to deflate their imaginary power in our minds.) The first movement of *MA II*, "Egoes Wars," starts off with the burning reds of Alex Wing's firestorm electric guitar, driven by my raging electronics and JoVia Armstrong's percussion. Our human world continues to be rife with slavery, neocolonialism, incarceration, forced prostitution, and economic inequities that fuel crime, terrorism, war, and massive suffering. I see a global practice of chewing up environmental resources to create money. I see our societies based too much on fake wealth (credit). I fear the world is on the verge of economic collapse. The western path is hitting a dead end. The heartbeat of Tatsu Aoki's taiko drum quickens in its call to battle. We all are witnessing Mama Earth's rage, as the climate of the Earth is in upheaval. There is massive desertification, where geographies once fertile and prosperous are now devoid of life, causing populations to starve, while

Nicole Mitchell Gantt

westernized cultures are experiencing an epidemic of diseases such as cancer, heart disease, and diabetes. The melismatic flutes of Kojiro Umezaki and myself and the strings of Tomeka Reid and Renée Baker plead unsuccessfully against the gravity of Alex Wing's burning guitar. Add to this (at the time of this writing) a raging pandemic that has made us sit our asses down so that Mama Earth can clean up our mess. Intended as a sonic dystopia, the music of "Egoes Wars" wails loudly over humanity's instability. With JoVia Armstrong's drums and my electronics thundering over Alex Wing's screeching guitar, "Egoes Wars" sonifies rage over the incredible denial of our ceaseless human destructiveness, which I visualize as humanity sleepwalking off the edge of a cliff. Like Mister Señor Love Daddy in Spike Lee's *Do the Right Thing*, I want to yell: "Yo! Hold Up! Time Out! Ya'll take a chill!"

I view our dystopic reality as a failure of the western system. While my creative aesthetic does not move me to write as an academic, and I have no background as a historian or cultural theorist to speak of, this project and my concern for humankind compelled me to dig for roots of what I call "the western problem." On this musically driven and philosophically idealistic search, my friend, cultural theorist Joshua Kun, pointed me toward Afro-Caribbean American philosopher and poet Sylvia Wynter, whose brilliant language and analysis brought much nutrition to my search. In *On Being Human as Praxis* Wynter writes:

> What at once becomes clear is this: rather than positing that "we humans have a poverty problem, or a habitat problem, or an energy problem, or a trade problem, or a population problem, or an atmosphere problem, or a waste problem or a resource problem," these on a planetary scale are understood, together, as "inter-connected problems."[11]

Wynter and countless others have done life's work on the task of illuminating "the western problem." If all these problems are connected, as Wynter explains so eloquently, what are the keys to solving them? Many of us today are finally realizing that this is a critical moment where we, as westerners, collectively need to open our eyes and really do something different. These failures of the western way of life are perpetuated by ideas that almost all of us walk around with in our heads. Of these ideas, one of the most destructive is *us vs. them*.

---

11   Katherine McKittrick, ed., *Sylvia Wynter: On Being Human as Praxis* (Durham, North Carolina: Duke University Press, 2015), 86.

One, two, three.

Can you take a moment and breathe with me?

One, two. Hold, and release.

Breathing helps us to stay centered and open.

I'm breathing with you.

I ask you to keep an open mind as you read, and observe your reactions as a way of us learning more about ourselves.

If you become uncomfortable, know that means there is something to gain.

Lean in.

Nicole Mitchell Gantt

Some of us are hungry. Some of us don't have clean water. In our daily lives, a message is reinforced through media, entertainment, and education. This message runs in the backs of our minds in contrast to the suffering around us. Some of us are targeted and killed because of being homeless or gay or Black. Yet the message that repeats in our minds is, "This is as good as it gets. western culture is the best." If you are living in a westernized region, I'm sure you are probably thankful to be living in what's considered a great place to be, even with whatever current struggles you may have. Even if the lights are out for days after the storm and you're left without heat, or if you've lost your home to fire or flood and the insurance won't cover it, or if you're living in your car because the rent is too high, or if your relative died because of a lack of resources for medical care, or if you're drowning in student loan debt, "west is as good as it gets" echoes through your mind. This thought, "It can't get better than this," freezes too many of us from doing more. I call the *west is "best"* idea fictional because there are strengths in every way of life, whether western or otherwise, but non-western ways are almost always diminished or dismissed by westerners.

A number of influential scholars (including British historians Stanley Lane-Poole and Elizabeth Drayson, Italian historians Louis Mendola and Vincenzo Salerno, and American historians John Henrik Clarke, Samuel Parsons Scott, and Chancellor Williams) acknowledge that for more than two centuries there were key Moor/Saracen (North African) influences on the development of european systems and culture in Portugal, Italy, and Spain. Yet these non-european influences in europe have been minimized and/or erased from the education of the westernized general public. That's precisely because the pervasive *west is "best"* belief parallels another pervasive idea, that *white wealthy is "best"* (the standard everyone else is conditioned to strive toward and be compared against). How could racism be influential if the game-changing contributions of melanated non-europeans to western society were fairly acknowledged? How would racism be convincing if it was widely recognized that Indigenous American systems, including those of the Iroquois, Cherokee, and Delaware nations, were influential to the USA's conception of democracy and state sovereignty in its formation of the Constitution,[12] as

---

12   "Iroquois Constitution: A Forerunner to Colonists' Democratic Principles," *The New York Times*, June 28, 1987, https://www.nytimes.com/1987/06/28/us/iroquois-constitution-a-forerunner-to-colonists-democratic-principles.html.

documented by historian Bruce E. Johansen?[13]

Because ruling class european men have credited themselves with having solely invented what we consider to be the western world/way and because these folks set up the concept of whiteness as their race, white (rich, male, not gay) "supremacy" became a thing. Most of us are familiar with white "supremacy" as a system-ized belief that insinuates that white people, as a race, are superior to all others. The term *white "supremacy"* creeps around, infecting and affecting everything around us, yet so few would even admit to agree-ing with it. I replace the word *supremacy* with *hegemony* because white hegemony is a more accurate expression of the act and process of european-enforced global systematic colonialism. white hege-mony is the actual process of systemized white domination, which is continually enacted upon the world and maintained daily. The appearance of the word-made phrase and concept white hegemony looks as outright wrong and ridiculous as the act itself. Saying *white hegemony* minimizes the perpetuation of the *white "supremacist"* idea by not empowering the latter term in its repetition. I won't use it anymore in this writing!

In westernized society each person's physical attributes liter-ally define what others *believe* that person deserves or doesn't deserve in that society. white (male, not-gay, rich) hegemony has been systemized and is per-petually enforced by laws, culture, minds, and actions.

---

13   Bruce E. Johansen, "Debating the Origins of Democracy: Overview of an Annotated Bibliography," *American Indian Culture and Research Journal*, vol. 20, no. 2 (1996), 155–72. See also Bruce E. Johansen, "Notes on the "Culture Wars: More Anno-tations on the Debate Regarding the Iroquois and the Origins of Democracy," *American Indian Culture and Research Journal*, vol. 23, no. 1 (1999), 165–75.

Nicole Mitchell Gantt

Have we really thought about how stupid the premise for *white hegemony* is? Why should our appearance/culture *automatically* give some a higher (lower) position than others? To understand this better, let me tweak the standard definitions of two racial terms below, and you can tell me how it makes you feel. What if the media defined white as equal to lifelessness, deficient of color, and empty. What if the media defined black as angelic, pure, inclusive of all color, and rich?

Doesn't it seem jarring, senseless, and/or wrong to bend these words in a way that would compel negative stereotypes that might ultimately impact how race is interpreted, impacting individuals and whole groups of people? Don't all babies poop, crawl, and say "mama" no matter their race or economic conditions? So why should their location, status, gender, and/or physical attributes determine whether they grow up consistently protected and cherished by society or doomed to fight inferior treatment? The idea of white hegemony (an extension of the idea of royal blood) convinces too many people of european heritage to believe that they deserve to be in control of valuable resources or that they have the right to better treatment than anyone else.

What I say here does not subtract from the fact that there have been countless people (including some who happen to be white) fighting for liberation, civil rights, human rights, and the eradication of white hegemony all over the world. Yet after more than five hundred years, after a multitude of protests, movements for equity, and even wars for sovereignty, after laws have been changed and innumerable people have been jailed, beaten, and killed, **why is it still here?** westernized humanity continues to fail in dissolving the active white hegemony concept. The western way of life continues to be viewed as "advanced," although its global reign has not changed the reality that people don't treat each other any better than they have for thousands of years.

"Egoes Wars," *Mandorla Awakening II*, 2015. Image by Ulysses Jenkins.

Whose fault is it if a critical mass of people in a society has severely limited access to food, education, or a life of comfort? What are the TRUE parameters of advancement and progress? How can I make art that expresses these concerns?

In the *Mandorla Letters*, when I say *western*, I'm referring to economic systems and cultural lifestyles that practice industrialization, digital technology, corporatization, media/pop culture, monoagriculture, and a processed food diet.

I myself am western/westernized. I empathize with communities across the world that desire and assert themselves to attain the seductively advertised western comforts of the so-called modern world. As Sylvia Wynter voices the west's seductive beckoning for the so-called Third World to join it, she says, "Oh, well, no longer be a native but come and be Man like us! Become homo *economicus*!"[14] My ancestors had a choice—be westernized or die—and they chose to live. For generations, they endured the US system of forced slavery on African people and the colonization of Indigenous Americans. In the process of westernization, generations of my family suffered. My ancestors lost their languages, cultures, geographical origins, Earth-centered lifestyles, and connection to our lineages. I mourn as I witness the continuous and further erasure of ancient systems of human wisdom, the loss of mother tongues, the toxification of crystalline waters, and the destruction of forests and fertile lands throughout the planet, all for the western way.

In present times, westernization remains a dominant focus for communities across the entire planet. Historically, western culture has not upheld human diversity as an asset. Through entertainment and news media, it has consistently cast negative shadows on non-western, non-white, non-male, non-wealthy, and gender non-binary people in service to white hegemony. However, westernization has affected (infected) much of the globe by facilitating the erasure (and erosion) of cultural

---

14   McKittrick, ed., *Sylvia Wynter*, 20.

and planetary diversity through monoculture and monoagriculture. Again, I point to Wynter's brilliant language on the subject. She states,

> The [w]est, over the last five hundred years, has brought the whole human species into its hegemonic, now purely secular (post-mono-theistic, post-civic monohumanist, therefore, itself also transump-tively liberal monohumanist) model of being human.[15]

The internet has only intensified and quickened this global trans-formation. Twenty-first-century colonization, what I call *i-colonialism*, comes at the cost of the destruction of countless ancient knowledge systems passed on through oral and apprentice traditions over thou-sands of years. The difference is that today's neocolonialism is not forced upon people but desperately desired by most of the converted. The majority of us who give up our older way of life for a shiny new one believe that joining the western world will be of great benefit. The electric-ity and digital connectivity spread under i-colonial rule, promises improve-ment in the fields of education, employment, and medical resources.

While there have been clear successes in these areas, western-ized geographies also generate a high ratio of waste with little to no accountability for it. There is massive environmental waste every-where. Off the coasts of California and Hawaii, there is an island of 600,000 square miles. It's bigger than some countries—and formed entirely of human-made garbage. It's a plastic mass (mess) born of western ways.[16] Does that exemplify advancement? The Water Protec-tors of Standing Rock are being disrespected and villainized for trying to safeguard the Earth's natural resources for all people. Human waste from westernized communities is causing disease, filth, starvation, and the extinction of countless plant and animal species. In May 2018, Damian Carrington, reporting for *The Guardian*, gave the following breakdown of life on our planet owing to westernized human activity:

Birds–poultry = 70%; wild birds = 30%

Mammals–livestock = 60%; humans = 36%; wild animals = 4%[17]

---

15   McKittrick, 20.

16   Doyle Rice, "World's largest collection of ocean garbage is twice the size of Tex-as," *USA Today*, March 22, 2018, https://www.usatoday.com/story/tech/science/2018/03/22/great-pacific-garbage-patch-grows/446405002/.

17   Damian Carrington, "Humans just 0.01% of all life but have destroyed 83% of wild mammals—study," *The Guardian*, May 21, 2018, https://www.theguardian.com/environment/2018/may/21/human-race-just-001-of-all-life-but-has-destroyed-over-80-of-wild-mammals-study.

What, what? All wild animals on the ENTIRE planet make up only 4% of all mammals?! Chickens, domestic turkeys, pigs, cattle, and so on comprise the majority of all—ALL!—living things (other than plants, wild birds, and sea life)? Are you KIDDING me? This is an example of what humanity has collectively agreed to embrace as advanced western civilization.

Within western systems, much talent is wasted. Many People of Color and low-income white people around the globe, if supported, could be offering solutions to some of these western failures, but, on the whole, they are not given the economic or educational opportunities to have an impact. This results in a continual collective loss of human potential that could be helping to solve world problems. I bring all this up because I believe we can do something about it.

OUR INVISIBLE THOUGHT-AGREEMENT

Spiritual teacher Don Miguel Ruiz, in his globally influential book *The Four Agreements*, writes that through assumptions based on what we see others do around us, we unconsciously support a reality that we've collectively agreed is unchangeable yet limiting. Yet our reality is changeable, and we each have the power to change it by first changing our thinking. The whole idea of *west is "best"* has been chiseled into our brains from childhood since the advent of colonialism more than five hundred years ago. Most westernized humans have collectively and unconsciously bought into what I call a western thought-agreement. Our actions are informed by the notion of western dominance, an idea that encapsulates all the intricacies of white hegemony, which stops us from looking for better. Even the simple words *up, down, left, right, white, black, dark,* and *light*—words that should have neutral value—are tainted with political associations because of our western thought-agreement. We can't drive a car making only right turns or we will not make it to our destination. On an airplane, we can't go up and never go down. We cannot have day without night. So, the binary judgements placed on these terms from our collective western thought-agreement literally *color* our reality with inaccuracies.

The idea of white hegemony is intrinsic to the western thought-agreement. The idea of white hegemony is reinforced with symbols and cues in conscious and unconscious repetition by the media, our education system, and the people around us.

Nicole Mitchell Gantt

As pervasive and seemingly unstoppable as it may seem, white hegemony is only mind-made, which means its power can also be extinguished by our minds.

Each of us has an individual choice whether to believe and support our western thinking or to revise it. The more of us who decide to believe something else, the less power it will hold. We can only act from what we know. I encourage us to revise our collective thought-agreements and empower more humane ideas.

Why does the meat-centered Burger King sell vegan burgers? Because thousands of individuals changed their views about their personal health and consciously altered their thought-agreement regarding what they ate; they decided to believe that a plant-based diet was better for them. This change, made by a critical mass of individuals, was enough to impact the collective western thought-agreement, thus compelling a multinational, billion-dollar corporation to revise its menu (or risk losing profits). That's collective power! In terms of eating, each of these thousands of individuals moved from unconscious action to conscious action, a key process to changing the thought-agreements to which we are bound.

Changing our thought-agreements can stimulate change. First, we become aware of what unconscious ideas are driving our actions. Then we revise our thought-agreements by replacing them with new ideas to change the actions of our lives.

MIND DE-COLONIZERS

The process of decolonizing our minds is daily work. As we revise our collective thought-agreements, we can empower more humane ideas.

Where will these more humane, non-hegemonic, antiracist, egalitarian ideas come from? We can only gain new understandings through a humble, open-minded quest to learn. We can only act from what we know. Some of the ideas with potential to positively shift the human narrative have been with us all along. We just might not be aware of them. It's encouraging to realize that there have been a multitude of incredible scholars, artists, teachers, scientists, and philosophers *outside* and within the western world who have worked tirelessly to analyze the design of white hegemony and to disempower it in their creations. They offer us pathways to decolonize our minds and new strands of thinking to weave into our revised thought-agreements. These are but a few limited examples:

- W. E. B. Du Bois's work, *The Souls of Black Folk*, is one of the earliest pathways of cultural theory. This book gave us the *veil* as a powerful metaphor for how Black and Indigenous people and People of Color are not ever quite seen for who we really are by westernized society, while not even truly seeing ourselves because of systemized racism.

- Psychiatrist Frantz Fanon offered us *Black Skin, White Masks* to illuminate in detail the self-hate embedded within nonwhite people as a result of our westernized (racialized) education and experience.

- Educator Paulo Freire's *Pedagogy of the Oppressed* reveals a process for liberation through gaining knowledge in order to recognize one's oppression and, with that knowledge, transform the system.

- In response to Freire's work, bell hooks offers us *Teaching to Transgress: Education as a Practice of Freedom*, where students' conscious transgressions against biases are encouraged and centralized within their educational process.

- In an example of the practical application of Freire's methods, educators Safisha and Haki Madhubuti have developed and maintained the Institute for Positive Education and a series of schools for more than fifty years, providing Chicago students with an African-centered education, pathways to seek knowledge-of-self, and a critical lens to understand the world.

- Information scientist Ron Eglash's book *African Fractals: Modern Computing and Indigenous Design* illuminates for westerners the mathematical genius of traditional African cultures, as the author develops a project he calls *generative justice* to shift western economics toward a more ethical and sustainable system.

- Charles Eisenstein, with *The More Beautiful World Our Hearts Know Is Possible*, calls for us to abandon our ideas of separation and realize our connectedness with all people and all beings on the planet, while inviting us to collaborate on new visions for a more equitable and sustainable world.

- adrienne maree brown, with her *Emergent Strategy: Shaping Change, Changing Worlds*, gives us practical tools for decolonizing our minds and organizing for positive change.

- Ibram X. Kendi's *How to Be an Antiracist* clarifies ways for people to act constructively toward improving racial equity.

- Aimé Césaire's *Discourse on Colonialism* flips the narrative of european hegemonic discourse to clearly expose flaws in western colonial ideology and action.

- Sylvia Wynter's transformational ideas in *Sylvia Wynter: On Being Human as Praxis* (edited by Katherine McKittrick) reveal a new framework for redefining humanity that opposes the present fractured, exclusive definitions of humanity based on race, gender, and class.

- In *Lo-TEK: Design by Radical Indigenism*, Julia Watson offers us a window into the genius innovations of indigenous, non-western sustainable architecture from India, Peru, the Philippines, Mexico, Brazil, Kenya, Iran, Benin, Iraq, New Mexico, Tanzania, and Indonesia.

- Jamika Ajalon illuminates the power that Women of Color hold to resist and eradicate dominant power structures in "FAR SPACE-WISE—Without Edges a Center Cannot Exist in Stasis" from the book *We Travel the Space Ways: Black Imagination, Fragments, and Diffractions* (edited by Henriette Gunkel and kara lynch).

- Robin Kelley's *Freedom Dreams: The Black Radical Imagination* provides encouragement for those of us seeking Black cultural optimism in a dystopic world.

- Ashon Crawley's *Lonely Letters* are at once intimate and exhaustive as he meditates on Black queer life and the transformative possibilities of joy found in music, love, and the Black Pentecostal church.

- Any of Fred Moten's writings will be a catalyst to disrupt our colonial programming, but especially *In the Break: The Aesthetics of the Black Radical Tradition*, which ornately testifies to the radical nature of Black American culture through the works of Duke Ellington, Cecil Taylor, James Baldwin, and others.

- In *Freedom Is a Constant Struggle: Ferguson, Palestine, and the*

Foundations of Movement, Angela Y. Davis ties parallels between liberation movements across the globe, and shows us that collective organizing with an international consciousness is key to transforming society.

- Jayna Brown's *Black Utopias: Speculative Life and the Music of Other Worlds* seeks communal creation as a doorway to manifest new worlds where Black liberation is possible.

What does any of this have to do with music or art? I repeat: Our imaginations are powerful, and with them we can create alternative worlds, starting with the manifestation of new ideas. Mandorla Island is a raw, incomplete, and hopeful example of an alternative vision. We don't have to continue believing in and empowering the current western thought-agreement steeped in white hegemony. I call on the words of my friend Jamika Ajalon, an Afrofuturist writer and music producer, who states:

> As eccentric futurists, whose movement is not dictated via a static center, we move through and within space in a way that allows us the freedom to imagine new worlds where the unbelievable can and does happen. The discerning eye can sense complicity between the construction/deconstruction of difference and standardization in which past, present, and future are imagined and represented under majoriborg rule—a standardization that is designed to ensure certain "inevitable futures" in which hierarchies stay intact. The idea of futurism then takes on sinister connotations.[18]

Through individual and small group efforts, we can collectively build new narratives and concepts capable of reverberating throughout human consciousness. We can rupture static hierarchies and create foundations for new worlds.

---

18   Jamika Ajalon, "FAR SPACE-WISE—Without Edges a Center Cannot Exist in Stasis," in *We Travel the Space Ways: Black Imagination, Fragments, and Diffractions*, ed. Henriette Gunkel and Kara Lynch (Bielefeld, Germany: Transcript, 2019), 8:417.

March 20 — 2018

Hey Love,

Thanks for helping me with this. I really appreciate it. I thought if enough of us own up to the fact that we don't know what we are doing and believe there's a power bigger than all of us, maybe we can survive past the DEAD-line and come up with something real toward human well-being. Do you have any creative ideas to lend right now? It's urgent, because blood is spilling and we keep on walking that way.

Guuuuurl, it's all been urgent for a while. Most of us haven't done a thing. I feel like we're in this holding pattern and can't find our way out. Except those brave kids who've been going out protesting for weeks now. Shame on us. So whenever you get a chance to think on this, it's fine. I'm trying to get this idea going on for that arts collective, but I've been slow as hell. So busy with the menial shit to keep my job, but at least I have one. We need something positive to work on together either way. I hope your family is healthy and safe through all this. Clearly now, I think we all realize that humanity is unstable.

Blessings and Wellness,
xoxo
Shareese

PS I would love you all to come by the farm and hang with us sometime. We've got fresh vegetables and—most important—fresh air. We gotta take care of ourselves. The stores don't have the healthy stuff unless they take your whole check.

PROTEST MUSIC, FRIENDSHIP MUSIC

Mandorla Awakening II is a sonification and physical embodiment of the mandorla concept of overlapping wisdoms through the celebration of differing musical traditions within a coexisting array of authentic voices. *MA II* is also a creative challenge to the normalized view that *west is "best"* and it is a call for us to honor musical practices that have survived western erasure. The work of Kojiro Umezaki, Tatsu Aoki, JoVia Armstrong, and avery r. young in *MA II* illuminates musical spaces where the shakuhachi, taiko, shamisen, cajon, and Black gospel traditions communicate in friendship with each other and with more western instruments. These practices are learned through apprenticeship and experience rather than in academic settings. For Umezaki, learning the tradition of shakuhachi was an act of individuality and resistance to the increasing westernization he witnessed while growing up in Japan from the 1960s to the 1980s

Nicole Mitchell Gantt

before he came to the US. As a child born to a Danish mother and Japanese father, Umezaki felt that his engagement with traditional Japanese artforms as a person of mixed race allowed him to do something unique from his peers, while "exploring and challenging what it meant to be a citizen."[19]

Each musical tradition expressed within *MA II* is embodied by a musician and uniquely informs that person's identity. Tatsu Aoki identifies himself as a postwar Japanese immigrant, whose experience contrasts with that of prewar immigrants who lost land and their rights when forced into US internment camps from 1942 to 1946. Traditional Japanese music was Aoki's foundation, and jazz marked a departure from it. Growing up in Tokyo, he listened to 78s of Black American music and rock 'n' roll on his grandmother's Victrola. Aoki rebelled against his geisha arts training by joining underground experimental theater groups, which led him to jazz and free improv, and eventually attracted him to seek creative music in Chicago.

While Black Earth Ensemble's performance of *Mandorla Awakening II* uplifts non-western traditions, it also challenges traditionalism as a limiting concept and practice. I admit it is very western of me to use my compositions as a platform to simultaneously honor and resist traditionalism through stretching it, but part of why I do it is in symbolic defiance of the invisibility of women as leaders and composers in almost every music tradition, including jazz and all styles of western music. Women music practitioners are often heralded as vocalists, but they are, for the most part, underrecognized as instrumentalists and leaders in the development of every field of music I can think of. JoVia Armstrong is an incredible percussionist, who, like many rhythm section players, has selflessly contributed more to other people's projects than her own. I foresee her artistry as a composer and producer coming to greater prominence over the next few years. Renée Baker has trail-blazed innovations with her creative composition in music for more than a decade via her interdisciplinary opera projects and her unique scores for silent black-and-white films. Baker's Chicago Modern Orchestra Project is rare in that it equally features works based in both improvisation and composition. Tomeka Reid is an under-recognized improvisational leader of the cello whose prominence is steadily increasing. The four of us—Armstrong, Baker, Reid, and I—are all composers, bandleaders, and AACM members. By taking agency over my voice as a composer, and including a critical mass of badass women in Black Earth

---

19   Kojiro Umezaki, email message to author, March 12, 2021.

Ensemble, I move to physically and sonically counteract the lack of acknowledgement of women leaders in the music field.

With *Mandorla Awakening II*, the act of making compositional decisions that might cause friction with traditionalist listeners was worth whatever rejection or ridicule it might incite. For strict traditionalists of Japanese culture, *MA II* might be considered offensive because it could be viewed as aligning the sounds of war/theater (taiko drum) with folk songs (shamisen) and temple music (shakuhachi) all within one musical space. However, all these instruments have played active roles in new, westernized experimental settings for decades. Aoki's annual Chicago project *Reduction* is a melding of contemporary experimental music practices with traditional taiko, infused with storytelling, dance, intricate costuming, and set design. Presented by Chicago's Museum of Contemporary Art, *Reduction* centers on a choreographed series of dramatic improvisational meetings between Asian diasporic artists and AACM musicians, where the presence of the unique physical instruments on stage is just as impactful as the sounds they make. Aoki's longstanding innovations with taiko in jazz contexts was a direct inspiration for me to include his voice in *MA II*.

Historically, the African American church tradition, jazz music, blues, and even the American banjo tradition are all close relatives of the same Black lineage, so one might assume a harmonious coexistence between these musics that I present in *Mandorla Awakening II*. That ain't necessarily the case. From the start of jazz and blues history, there was a contingent of religious Black folk who enforced the belief that all music should only be in *praise of the Lord*. To them, jazz and other non-worship music, Black or otherwise, was historically considered the *work of the devil*. Artists like W. C. Handy, Ray Charles, Malachi Favors, Aretha Franklin, and even Mr. avery r. young, all of whom applied their church-honed musical skills to secular music, have had these folks shaking their heads in disappointment. Today, this contingent is small and dwindling. Thankfully, young, who grew up in a Baptist home, was openly encouraged by his mother's love to share his God-given talents in any form he chooses. He testifies,

> There is nothing within me that doesn't feel blessed by the manner of blk I grew up as. Being raised inside a culture milieu of blackness on the West Side of Chicago. The accessibility to sinner and saint one can gather on a Sunday afternoon walking past the church that's a couple of

Nicole Mitchell Gantt

doors down from the liquor store and/or tavern. I call it Sunday morning jook-joint. That part when Shug Avery is standing in the middle of the church. The jook jointers and holy rollers talking about God is trying to tell you something! And literally in that moment God is trying to tell us that they see all as children. No bad child or good child. Just children who do what they do in the midst of various circumstances and realities. We. People. We the people divide. God multiplies![20]

These musical languages of the Black church, Japanese culture, and even the banjo are symbolic embodiments of living traditions considered to be non-european (non-western). Tomeka Reid has been excited to join the increasing number of Black women currently playing the banjo in celebration of its African roots.[21] Moreover, all these instruments are avatars of my friends, and my friends are activators of these diverse traditions and are people I value. They come from different experiences and directly enrich my life. *MA II* represents courage and community among the players to celebrate unique traditions while we also collectively break those traditions in the music, like breaking bread. Why not model a real community of friendship through sound?

20   avery r. young, email message to author, March 11, 2021.

21   Tomeka Reid, email message to author, March 12, 2021.

"Dance of Many Hands," *Mandorla Awakening II*, 2015. Musical score by Nicole Mitchell.

Entry 2.

It's me again, Dorla. I'm sure WU doesn't know about this place. But even I wouldn't want them to know.

They would definitely try to destroy it and take all the assets. They might even kill everyone here. The folks here talk a lot about this "mindlake" or "dreamswimma." They say there's a pathway through mindwrap. Mindwrap. Is that how we got here? I wish I could see a map. I don't totally get this stuff because it's so abstract. I remember hearing about dreamwalking before, from a book about the original humans of Australia. But even the aborigines were seduced by WU a generation ago, once they started drinking pop and eating sugar cereal like everybody else. Eating that junk seems to have hurt their connection with the land—and quickly. A lot of them started to get sick. They stopped hunting and started getting all the diseases we get—high blood pressure, diabetes, cancer. I wonder if it's the food we eat that defines our bodies and spirits. Maybe what we eat even affects how we think? Last I heard they came onto the grid with everyone else. They wanted, they needed education for their kids. Now, almost all the remote areas are on the grid. Except those people that walked out of WU. Good luck to them out there with the vigilantes. Those people refused to wear the WU tags and left the gates to survive in the violence out there. I haven't heard from my cousin in years. He's out there somewhere. Hope he's still alive. I thought living in WU was the best possible life. But seeing this place, I don't know. These people actually know their parents! They seem happy.

I was thinking about it, and actually we don't even know if we're AI clones at this point. How

Ha, that would be deep, if we're not even real people. How would we know? But, here, on this Mandorla Island, everyone has relationships with their families, and ages aren't separated. Makes you wonder, what have we been missing? Also, it's kind of a mystery how the government works here. It just seems like networks of families working together for what they need. I haven't seen any police at all, but everyone is so in sync. You should see their tech! That's the whole thing—you can't see it! The people appear and disappear. How would you catch someone like that for a crime anyway? It's not clear how this place works. It's deep.

TOGETHER/ NOT TOGETHER

Everyone has their own way of breathing, dancing, seeing, moving, and talking. Each instrument has its own textural qualities. The fingers and breath that play instruments are completely unique. Yet there is a beauty almost universally appreciated when different elements/bodies come together in a symbolic expression of unity. Coming together illuminates human understanding of commonalities and connections. *Together/not together* is a musical term that I call a *niki*-ism, or something core to my personal compositional aesthetic. I feel a power in hearing two or more instruments moving together in a unison musical phrase, perhaps because it symbolically expresses unity. And yet, as a person, I don't enjoy following the leader, and I don't like to do the same thing as someone else, especially when I'm told to. After all, the *my way or the highway* mindset is core to

Nicole Mitchell Gantt

western thinking. Rather, I'm moved by the playfulness of butterflies dancing in similar motion, empathetic to one another yet each expressing a unique individuality. There is a call-and-response utilized by most wildlife in nature. Birds return another's song in their reply, as if to say, "I hear you!" but with added embellishments. And so, *together/not together* is a way for us as musicians to play a similar statement, while overlapping our voices imperfectly, so that each texture and individual is heard.

Together/not together expresses my sense of coexistence in diversity. Rather than the "melting pot" concept of the '70s, where people were expected to give up their ways of being (assimilate) to reach an impossible white standard, diversity coexistence is about people being respected for their differences as they are. In "Dance of Many Hands," movement 4 of *MA II*, three treble instruments—my flute, Renée Baker's violin, and Kojiro Umezaki's shakuhachi—freely dance through a similar melody, overlapping and gently pulling against one another's rhythm and sense of tempo. The clarity of expression of *together/not together* can be layered atop a foundational groove, just as the ground and trees are rooted and give context for the butterflies to dance in the wind. Alex Wing's guitar and Tomeka Reid's cello circle each other, playing the same phrase, slightly displaced, to create a groundwork with JoVia Armstrong's bouncing rhythms to support the flight of our treble instruments. One of my greatest *together/not together* moments of sonic joy is the firefly flute dance that happens between myself on western flute and Ko Umezaki on shakuhachi in "Mandorla Island" (movement 9 of *MA II*). Long gestures flutter and vibrate to build a sonic vision of a utopian island. Metal and bamboo coexist in unity by way of the human breath that animates these flutes, representing the merging/overlapping of western and Earth-based materials to create new ways of being.

I've experienced a powerful organizational embodiment of *together/not together* as a member of the Association for the Advancement of Creative Musicians (AACM). While the musician-composers of the AACM are together in sharing overlapping experiences of Black cultural heritage, a key to the success and impact of the collective is that we also support one another being *not together*. The AACM's strength lies in its members' personal artistic visions and pursuits. Rather than hailing one signature musical approach for all, the group heralds the uniqueness of each and provides support for individual artistic exploration and experimentation. I believe that one of the AACM's greatest achievements has been in providing the tools for liberating Black minds. There aren't too many primarily Black institutions in the world that maintain a social environment designed specifically to encourage its members to think creatively. The list of innovations coming out of the AACM seems almost infinite. Henry Threadgill developed his own highly sophisticated and soulful compositional form for improvising ensembles. George E. Lewis taught computers how to improvise. Roscoe Mitchell developed new improvisational languages for the saxophone. Mike Reed found new business models for the prosperity of creative music in live venues and at festivals. Renée Baker created new approaches to film scoring. Amina Claudine Myers integrated experimental and Black gospel approaches to the Hammond organ. Wadada Leo Smith developed a new system of musical notation. These are but a few examples of *together/not together* inspired by the AACM.

November 16 — 2018

What up, Sis Shareese,

Was so good to see you last summer. Loved those mustard greens and strawberries! I feel what you've been talking about. Stuff is happening everywhere now and all at the same time. In the last month, there were two mass shootings— one over here in SoCali and one in Pittsburgh. Devastating. That makes 307 mass shootings in 2018! I read it in *USA Today*. As if that wasn't enough, did you hear about the fires in California? Burned down over a million acres and killed over a hundred! Then there's the hurricanes— Puerto Rico and North Carolina. The news ain't even covering it! And Flint's drinking water stilllllllll hasn't been cleaned up. You're talking about thousands of people, mostly Black folk, paying a water bill that's killing them. They literally can't drink it! I know you got fam over there in Detroit. Are they OK? And the police killings won't stop. Don't get me started. Over where you are in Paris, I heard a number of world leaders met who were just too through with that man of the white house in their midst. Please travel safe home. (And bring me something.)

James Baldwin said there would be "the fire next time." Well......it looks like it's about that time. He wasn't kidding. Humanity is unstable. You've been saying that for years. It seems kinda insensitive at this point to remind folks of Baldwin's words, because now we IN IT.

To be honest, do you feel helpless? This moment is horrific. If you look at it globally, as a human species, we don't care about each other and we definitely don't care about nature. Isn't that a suicidal tendency by default?

But don't worry, I still got a few drops of optimism left.

What about you? How was your exhibit at the museum? Doesn't art, right now, seem so "inessential"? Like playing basketball during an epidemic? Not to take away from your amazing work. You making a difference. I'm just trying to pay my rent right now. They raised it another $200 again. Anywho, I'm gonna go dance my heart out and jump some rope to Ras G and Afrikan Space Program's sunshine spaceship beats right now.

We livin our best liiiiifffffe (ain't goin back and forth…)!

TTYL,
Deondra

THE SILOS OF HIERARCHY

While in the development phase of *Mandorla Awakening II*, I directed a video shoot of people struggling on a staircase, choreographed by Sheron Ama Wray, with camerawork by Ulysses Jenkins. Each actor in the scene was trying to get to the top of the stairs. They were only thinking about themselves. In a volatile competition, they pushed and even knocked others out of the way to get to the top, with no regard for the harm their actions caused. Each fought to be *first* at any cost, with no sense of connection to the others. In life, no one wants to be at the bottom, because those at *the bottom* have the least power and fewest/worst choices. Those at the top have the best circumstances and are conceived to be *winners*. While the "Staircase Struggle" scene (movement 7 of *MA II*) was made to be humorous, it symbolized my visualization of the downsides of hierarchical thinking. The idea of being first is deeply embedded in western lifestyles

Nicole Mitchell Gantt

at every level. Some people travel first class, while others compete for first place or top recognition in their field, whether it be sports, entertainment, science, the corporate sector, or music. Being *first* almost always means having more money and options than others. As children, we are taught early on about the importance of *winning* from the likes of spelling bees, athletic meets, and board games, and this concept is affirmed everywhere. The *winner* gets the *prize* and no one else. When it's someone's birthday, they come first.

Hierarchy is central to the infrastructure of most corporations, universities, and government institutions where there are levels of power from least to most. While I respect the need for effective organizational structures, and I agree that hierarchical structures have been successful on many *levels* (haha), it seems to me that the *winner* mindset is overvalued in western culture. In western societies, too often, being a winner (usually through capital gain) is prioritized over collective well-being. There is a level of *firstness* that can be destructive, especially if the essential human rights of many are sacrificed so that a select few can enjoy exclusive privileges.

Where did this hierarchical thinking that's so prevalent in western society come from? Marimba Ani's book *Yurugu: An African-Centered Critique of European Cultural Thought and Behavior* reveals several key european thought-agreements that westerners are entangled in. Ani analyzes Plato's design for european society in the *Republic*, explaining that it is so deeply entangled in our society's language that it is difficult for us to diverge from it. To illuminate Ani's ideas, let's get Platonic! We understand that in a platonic relationship, a couple is not romantically involved. Ani explains that in Plato's epistemology, emotions and physical intimacy are relegated to the lower "bad" self, while intellect is relegated to the higher "good" self. So, to be platonic (Platonic) is to be cerebral. To be non-emotional and "intellectual" is heralded by western leadership as "superior." To be emotional, or to use the senses or intuition, is discouraged and compared to being like an "animal" (and Plato defines animals as "inferior" to people). Since people (mammals!) are born with a wide emotional capacity and are never free of emotions, humans are viewed as intrinsically flawed. Therefore, the western view of being human is that it is the condition of being split between good and bad parts that are in a constant inner battle. Command/control becomes the focus of one's life as a westerner—to control one's self and surroundings. Seeking control of the environment and other people (ethnic groups, religious groups, nations) has been the western way.

With this "logic," europeans defined Africans and non-westerners as being more intuitive, mysterious, and emotional than white people so that they could justify stealing land, precious metals, diamonds, oil, and even people from Africa, Asia, the Americas, the Caribbean islands, and Australia.

In western culture, so-called intellectuals are placed on *top* because they *appear* to best control their emotions and therefore "have command" of themselves. The concept of *supremacizing* Platonic ideals (separating the self into bad and good parts) is foundational to the erroneous hierarchical framework that has been normalized—a framework where men are positioned above women through the justification of men being defined as more logical (lies!) and women as more emotional (lies!). Gay and/or queer people complicate the broadly erroneous assumptions of this gender binary. Humans are positioned hierarchically above all other animals (and all of nature) because animals, in western thought, are not considered to be *thinking* beings, and so on. Plants, within this framework are seen as *things* to make use of, not *beings* to respect. None of these ideas are factual; they are theories normalized and embedded into western frameworks.

Hierarchical thinking, the idea of some(one) being more deserving of power than others, is massively institutionalized and supported by popular culture.

Ani also astutely points to Plato's concept of objectivity as the groundwork for european scientific thought that ultimately empowered western societal design. For the old Trekkies out there, we can think of Mr. Spock. Mr. Spock is half-human and half-Vulcan. His Vulcan side endows him with clear-cut reason. For him, everything is about the *facts*; his most famous phrase is "That's highly illogical." In western science, proof must be based on *object*ive facts and physical evidence. But for something to be wholly based on objective facts, everything one studies must be considered an *object*. What I find funny is how, when people make life decisions, sure, they consider the facts, but at the end of the day, they often just go with how they *feel in their* gut. Spock would call that "illogical." The concept of an *intelligent gut* lacks validity in western society, but it's quite real in African and non-western societies. The gut is one's inner wisdom, in alignment with the universe or God. In western society, everything is an object—people, places, and things! All *things* considered (pardon the irony), thoughts themselves are defined as things. People are also objectified, and in most of our westernized relationships, whether intimate or business-related, we often witness competition, with one person trying to control the other(s).

In traditional African and other, non-western cultures, knowledge is not objective; rather, to know is to sense truth in every part of one's being. Everything is subjective because it is informed by real experience. Trees, places, and people are all living beings that are too complex to look at as objects. Plato, in his writings, makes the case that *objectivity* is the only *true* way to perceive reality, but—as Ani's writing illuminates—in *fact* (to use Spock logic), objectivity itself is an illusion. Ani's analysis brilliantly reveals how Plato played a trick on us all—how he was, in fact, a type of magician (like the Yoruba deity, Elegba). With his imagination, he created a theoretical reality (his utopic vision) that eventually manifested into a future—our physical reality. Plato is one of the great architects of the western mindset. His ideas have greatly influenced the system of embedded silos and struggles based on gender, class, race, beliefs, and our separation from nature. But, as Ani wrote, because we are so immersed in western thought, how do we fully see this error in order to change the patterns of our lives? To quote Audre Lorde, "You can't use the master's tools to dismantle the master's house."

UNWRAPPING POSITION- ALITIES

I was traveling home from a music tour in Paris. I had just "achieved" priority status with my airline a few days before, but my flight happened to be managed by a partner airline that did not acknowledge my priority status. After almost twenty minutes moving slowly through the economy line, I was targeted by security and told to go back and check my bag. Whenever I'm stopped by security, I often wonder if it is because of my melanated skin. My bag was smaller than those of other passengers who happily whisked through the line while I was detained. As a musician, I was carrying several pounds of very delicate equipment that absolutely could not be checked as baggage. In any case, I would surely have missed my

Nicole Mitchell Gantt

flight if I had gone to check it. Instead of following instructions, I headed to the check-in desk of the airline where I had just established elite status. I asked for a reprint of my ticket with the priority designation made clear. This was all I needed to magically glide through the priority security line (with no weight restrictions) and make my flight. If I hadn't achieved elite status because I was a frequent flyer, I would certainly have missed my flight.

There is explicit privilege in this story. I achieved the status of an internationally renowned musician with continual opportunities to perform around the globe. I am guilty of contributing to a negatively large carbon footprint because, until recently, my work had gained greater recognition in europe than in my home country. My life has been full of wins, the result of hard work, but also of pervasive aspects of hierarchy that are truly not equitable—my appearance and my economic privilege. I am a light-skinned Black woman with a small, nonthreatening voice and a generally optimistic attitude raised in a lower-middle-class family with both parents. I did not grow up hungry, and the light bill was always paid.

Intersectional analysis, thanks to the writings of Kimberlé Crenshaw, can help us understand our positionalities and where we may take our privileges for granted. Each of us has a complex, nonbinary identity based on our physical attributes, gender, sexuality, wealth, access to education, and cultural background that translates into our lived experience of complex relationships with power in society. The hierarchical thinking of society positions all Brown and Black folks, because of our appearance, as targets of discrimination throughout our lifetimes. As a child, because of my racial position, white children and adults frequently picked fights with me. One unforgettable day, a group of neighborhood white boys chased me with ropes, yelling, "Come here, Kizzie!" while trying to whip me like they saw in the movie *Roots*. In hope of safety, I scurried up to the nearest adult. "Help me!" I pleaded. The man looked down at me, hands in his pockets, and smirked. Time stopped as I realized this man was a father to one of the boys in the pack that was terrorizing me. This was my first encounter with a policeman in uniform. My young self could not understand how people could hate me for breathing—literally, just existing. Being Black in America (North, Central, and South America) is an abusive relationship that you are born into and cannot escape. Yet it's the only home we've got.

On one side of intersectionality, Black people in the US are collectively one of the wealthiest groups of Black people in the world, but on the flip side, the median household income for Black families continues to be lower than that of any other racial group.[22] Within my racial positionality, I experience the complexity of being yellow-Black. While both my parents were Black American, my father, of lighter hue, was referred to by the racists on the block as American, while my mother was referred to as a "darky." In my child's mind, this was puzzling, because I knew my mother was just as American as my father; they were born in the US, as were their parents, and their parents, and so on. It made zero sense to me that only white-looking people were considered American, when Indigenous people lived in America first, and we, like many Black Americans, according to my grandparents, had Indigenous blood in our veins.

My father never denied being African American. He grew up on the Black side of the tracks in Kalamazoo, Michigan, but if no one asked, he let them assume what they wanted. His lighter skin and work ethic positioned him with an engineering degree and opportunities for employment, which I learned was easier because of his racially ambiguous appearance (perhaps he was Arab or Italian or Jewish?). This helped him ascend from the poverty he grew up in. The benefits he attained ultimately positioned me and my brothers to grow up in an economically stable, albeit hostile neighborhood. I recognize that my inherited white-adjacent looks, my decent education, my ability to subtract Ebonics from my speech, and perhaps even an ancestral memory that causes me to slide into occasional expressions of house negritude have all contributed to my acceptance by white people, who mostly do not feel threatened by my presence and might even find me likable.

As a Black woman, I've asked myself why I've found it more difficult to articulate the complexities of my struggle regarding gender than those concerning race. What I realized is that a lot of work that Black women, including myself, do to improve gender equity is within the Black community, but unlike the work for racial equity, which is often recognized and heralded publicly, the work for gender equity within the Black community is often invisible work because we as Black women have a seemingly ancestral impulse to protect Black men. So, while we struggle with Black men to increase equity in Black spaces, that work is often ignored or under-recognized by Black men, while it's mostly unknown in public spaces. Yet this work

---

22   John Creamer, "Inequalities Persist Despite Decline in Poverty For All Major Race and Hispanic Origin Groups," United States Census Bureau, September 15, 2020, https://www.census.gov/library/stories/2020/09/poverty-rates-for-blacks-and-hispanics-reached-historic-lows-in-2019.html.

takes up immeasurable space in our minds and countless hours of our time in conversations and strategizing. A great inspiration to me is drummer/composer/educator Terri Lyne Carrington, who founded the Institute of Jazz and Gender Justice at Berklee College of Music. Carrington takes real action to further gender equity and increase respect for, and contributions from, women in jazz music. For the first time in jazz history, gender justice in jazz has become a significant public conversation on a national scale. Carrington's work has been key to that shift.

With the help of my very woke friend, the vocalist and scholar Imani Uzuri, I have recently come to realize that, like my father, I have also let people make assumptions about me that advantage my navigation in society. Though I openly acknowledge there may be undeserved perks of being lighter-skinned, over the years I have allowed others to assume that I am straight, when I am, in fact, attracted to people regardless of their gender identity. Because I have a history of long monogamous relationships with men, and I've been happily married to a beautiful man I love very much for more than a decade, these politics of appearance allow for me to be invisible as a queer person. That's an unfair privilege that others don't have. In the process of realizing how I've minimized this part of myself, I've also remembered crucial threads of my artistic life, exploring queerness, that have been pushed out of the story I've shared with others. Most importantly, by shaming or ignoring this part of myself, I've neglected analysis of the powerful role that queerness can have shaping positive alternative worlds. As José Esteban Muñoz writes, queerness may be the very aspect of life that offers insight toward improved social relations:

> Turning to the aesthetic in the case of queerness is nothing like an escape from the social realm, insofar as queer aesthetics map future social relations. Queerness is also a performative because it is not simply a being but a doing for and toward the future. Queerness is essentially about the rejection of a here and now and an insistence on potentiality or concrete possibility for another world.[23]

In 1991, just before cofounding Samana (the first all-women group of the AACM) with multi-instrumentalists Shanta Nurullah and Maia, I cofounded a Black feminist collective with Cuban American poet Teresa Vazquez and poet/musician Jamika Ajalon that explored

---

23   Muñoz, *Cruising Utopia*, 1.

queerness, Blackness, and womanhood through poetry and music. All in our early twenties, we created WomanFireSpirit, which was perhaps the most radical performance collective of the many that I would be involved in throughout my career. Ajalon and Vazquez were the first friends that made me not feel that I was strange or alone in the world, because we all had intriguingly parallel perceptions of life and wanted to use our creative abilities for resistance to societal limitations.

This time period was also when I was most actively involved in intimate relationships with women, and the three of us were part of a wider circle of friends that was openly supportive of queerness. Over time, this circle dissipated, as everyone moved on toward our later twenties, but WomanFireSpirit remains a critical juncture of my artistic development, and the three of us remain good friends.

Teresa Vazquez was born the same day as my deceased mother, JBM. We met and became friends when we were students at Oberlin College. Vazquez was living in Chicago, which made my move there in 1990 easier. Jamika Ajalon and I were born on the same day, a year apart, and met in Chicago just after I arrived. We immediately became soul sisters. Jamika was studying experimental film at Columbia College at the time. The three of us enjoyed conversations about poetry, music, culture, spirituality, sexuality, relationships, and politics, which made each of us feel heard. There was a fearlessness in this celebration of Black feminism that our synergy as creatives inspired in all of us.

In WomanFireSpirit, Teresa was the erotic one (Woman); she fearlessly expressed sexual experiences and intimacy through her poetry in ways that made me blush. Jamika was the liberated one (Fire); she expressed her queerness and critiques of the system through her poetry with total courage. I was the intuitive one (Spirit). I saw myself as less confident than my comrades, but I spoke my truth through flute, beats, and poetry exploring spirituality, womanhood, Black feminism, and identity. Our premiere of the WomanFireSpirit project was at Chicago's Women & Children First bookstore in Lincoln Park, which serendipitously landed us a review in *The New Yorker*.

I ask myself, why, in all these years, haven't I credited this trio, WomanFireSpirit, as a crucial group I was involved in at the start of my artistic path in Chicago until now? It is unquestionable that this chapter of my history with Ajalon and Vazquez was essential to the development of my artistic and philosophical motivations in Black Earth Ensemble and, most definitely, in *Mandorla*

Awakening. Was it because of my unconscious patriarchal leanings, and/or homophobia? The process of writing this book, as a quest toward colliding our dystopic world with utopian-informed possibilities, has also been a process of unveiling hidden truths even to myself.

RIGHT IS OF NO SEX. TRUTH IS OF NO COLOR.

(FREDERICK DOUGLASS, 1847, *THE NORTH STAR*)

One cold, slushy Chicago day in 1990, Jamika Ajalon and I took the 'L' train down to 79th Street, and walked past Black beauty shops, kiddie cares, currency exchanges and a funeral home, to sign up as interns for Haki Madhubuti's publishing company, Third World Press (TWP). There we discovered that the majority of Black writers that submitted manuscripts to be considered for publishing were overly focused on reflections of lived past experiences, retaining Black history, and critiquing/perpetuating Black trauma throughout history. We saw that there were very few writers at the time who were imagining what *could be*. As young artists, Jamika and I both believed that it was our calling to make visionary work, to create alternative worlds. I would stay with TWP as a graphic designer for more than a decade, soaking up African-centered mentorship from the cultural community that Baba Haki fostered. Jamika, who recog-

Nicole Mitchell Gantt

nized the homophobic limitations of the Chicago Afrocentric community, eventually left TWP. The fact that I could remain to grow in the Afrocentric community and take in the legacy of the Black Arts Movement, in toleration of its homophobia, while my friend Jamika could not, speaks partly to my appearance-positionality of passing as straight. I didn't feel targeted but—if only sharing my partial self to this community—was I free?

All of us, whether conscious of it or not, experience specific treatment by others based on our appearance-positionality in the society we live. We also react to others based on our society-influenced judgments about their beauty, color, body shape, smell, cultural gestures, dialect, and/or what they are wearing. Sadly, our reactions to others and even ourselves are too often based on the collective thought-agreement (mainstream ideas) of our community, and in many cases, this is the perpetuation of white hegemony.

MONEY CAN'T BUY US SAFETY

Appearance-positionality is a crucial flaw in our present human consciousness. For Black and Brown folks in the un-United States and around the globe, the positive experiences of our culture and family life are inevitably infused with the poison of the physical and psychological racial violence experienced outside (and sometimes inside) the home. Yet, in spite of these experiences, for me and most Black folks I know, to be of African heritage is a gift of cultural wealth that we wouldn't trade for anything. A hundred years ago, anthropologist and Harlem Renaissance artist Zora Neale Hurston, in "How It Feels to Be Colored Me," shared some of her earliest experiences of racism, and concluded,

> ...but I am not tragically colored. There is no sorrow dammed up in my soul, nor lurking behind my eyes. I do not mind at all.... No, I do not weep at the world—I am too busy sharpening my oyster knife.[24]

---

24   Zora Neale Hurston, "How It Feels to Be Colored Me," *World Tomorrow* (1928), 215–16.

Nicole Mitchell Gantt

We can't ignore the fact that western culture consistently manifests a continued assault on Black people and other People of Color through the violent words, violent acts, and violent laws of its individuals, groups, and institutions. Hierarchical thinking can cause someone in a privileged position to look down on another's appearance or beliefs (religious or political) and decide that this other human is *not one of us*. Too often, the police are called, and brutality (often on the innocent) ensues, no questions asked. The hegemonic violence supported by the western system is real and it can be carried out with a quickness.

The idea that what someone looks like should determine a person's value and importance over others is one of the greatest philosophical limitations on our human identity and behavior.

Anti-Black violence is directed at Black people literally because of physical attributes (skin color, hair texture, facial features) that are defined as "opposite" of those of white people positioned at the top of the hierarchy. (What's ridiculous about this is that Black folks have incredible diversity in our skin color, hair texture, and facial features, as do white folks, and people of every other culture!) Historically, the media and the education system has consistently (and wrongfully) associated the appearance-positionality of Black and Brown folks with criminality through embedded stereotypes. Because of this criminalized appearance-positionality, the lived experience of Black and Brown people tells us that even in a system where wealth is equated with happiness (i.e., the American Dream), we know that money cannot buy us safety. Even with a loaded bank account, we are susceptible to targeting by police and catching hell in the form of discrimination, incrimination, violence, and microaggressions because of our appearance-positionality. Money isn't enough to make us "free."

I see this dystopic aspect of western hierarchical systems as one of the most important to be addressed for us to move forward into creating a world that truly loves all of us. I dream of futures where multitudes of groups, each manifesting great ideas for sustainable and equitable life, prioritize the dissolving of all hierarchical prejudices, especially those based on appearance. When we can understand how much it hurts us all, we can change it.

"Land Mandorlians," *Mandorla Awakening I*, 2013. Performance still. Choreography by Lisa Naugle. Costumes by Jeni Hayes-Presnall. Photo by Joel Wanek.

Nicole Mitchell Gantt

The process of decolonizing our minds is daily work.

In "Forestwall Timewalk" (movement 6 of *MA II*), the taiko and percussion repeat a menacing drum call to battle, while the electric guitar rampages into a dystopic melody, flailing in anger. A mournful choir of strings and flutes sonically lament in unison questions about humanicide, pleading higher and higher, while the guitar responds with a hurricane storm of destruction.

A family friend, in 2016, was held at gunpoint by five police officers in the Irvine suburbs because they thought he was burgling his family's home. At the time, the young man believed that because he had a white parent and economic privilege, he did not need to identify as Black. This and other experiences of harassment at the hands of police opened his eyes to the reality that there is no escape from the ugly racist legacy he was born into: his Blackness automatically makes him an immediate target for violence.

The vulnerable strings and flutes circle faster and faster seeking hope to no avail, then fall silent amid a violent frenzy of guitar. Finally, the guitar eruption acquiesces into lonely puckering teardrops. The violin is compelled to lament the destroyed.

In 2015, Lawrence Crosby, a PhD student at Northwestern University in Evanston, Illinois, shared with the *Washington Post* his experience of "driving while Black," which led to him being beaten, arrested, and accused of "stealing" his own car.[25]

Suddenly, avery r. young appears, singing emphatically:

We keep doing the same thing over and over again!

All the instrumental voices join together in a ritual of repetition, reaching and swirling upward toward the sky. The sounds rotate faster and faster, spinning out of control until an eruption that culminates in a solitary voice.

---

25   Lawrence Crosby, "Police attacked me for stealing a car. It was my own," *The Washington Post*, June 29, 2018, https://www.washingtonpost.com/opinions/police-attacked-me-for-stealing-a-car-it-was-my-own/2018/06/29/86829292-7658-11e8-b4b7-308400242c2e_story.html.

Ahmed Ag Kaedy of northern Mali was using his music as a message of liberation and peace when Islamic extremists threatened to cut off his fingers if he continued to play music in his hometown.[26]

(avery sings) Blood is spilling.

Sandra Bland changed lanes without using her turn signal, which ultimately resulted in her death while in custody in a Texas jail.

(avery sings) Blood is spilling, and we keep walking that way.

The Center for Public Integrity reported that the murder rate for Native American women is up to ten times higher than that for any other racial group of women in the United States, and that the majority of the culprits are white and non-Native American men.[27]

(avery) I know there's gotta be a better way.

Eric Garner was choked to death for selling single cigarettes outside a convenience store. Kevin Powell and Stephen Adams, targeted because they appeared to be gay, were brutally tortured and shot by a man who believed it was his right as a straight white man to "put them down."[28]

26   Joshua Hammer, "Along the Niger River, the Beat of the Sahel," *The New York Times*, January 15, 2015, https://www.nytimes.com/2015/01/18/travel/along-the-niger-river-the-beat-of-the-sahel.html.

27   Garet Bleir and Anya Zoledziowski, "Murdered and Missing Native American Women Challenge Police and Courts," The Center for Public Integrity, October 29, 2018, https://publicintegrity.org/politics/murdered-and-missing-native-american-women-challenge-police-and-courts.

28   Brooke Sopelsa, "Florida man to be executed for 'execution style killings' of gay couple," *NBC News*, August 31, 2018, https://www.nbcnews.com/feature/nbc-out/florida-man-be-executed-execution-style-killings-gay-couple-n905566.

(avery) This is not a story. People live it every day.

Jimmy Smith-Kramer, a young Native American, was mowed down and killed by a white man who drove his truck both forward and backward over Smith-Kramer's body.[29]

(avery) What do we do ya'll?

A million people were held in internment camps in China because the government viewed their religion, Islam, as a "pathology,"[30] while internment camps in the United States separated hundreds of immigrant children from their parents and held them in unlivable conditions.

(avery) I want to pick up my blade.

In the first three months of 2021, twelve transgender and gender nonconforming people were brutally murdered in the US.[31]

(avery) There's gotta be a better way.

Where is justice for Breonna Taylor, shot in her bed in Louisville while she slept? Ahmaud Arbery was jogging when targeted, shot, and killed. The killing of George Floyd erupted a volcano of protests and riots worldwide.

---

29 Rahima Nasa, "A White Man in a Truck Mowed Down a Young Native American Man. Was it a Hate Crime?" *Mother Jones*, April 27, 2018, https://www.motherjones.com/crime-justice/2018/04/a-white-man-in-a-truck-mowed-down-a-young-native-american-man-was-it-a-hate-crime/.

30 Sigal Samuel, "China Is Treating Islam Like a Mental Illness" *The Atlantic*, August 28, 2018, https://www.theatlantic.com/international/archive/2018/08/china-pathologizing-uighur-muslims-mental-illness/568525/.

31 "Fatal Violence Against the Transgender and Gender Non-Conforming Community in 2021," Human Rights Campaign, updated December 28, 2021, https://www.hrc.org/resources/fatal-violence-against-the-transgender-and-gender-non-conforming-community-in-2021.

There are too many examples to reflect on. This is so wrong. It's the very worst of what humanity can be.

Blood is spilling, and we just keep walking that way as if we are zombies, dead to the universal destruction we are causing. If human beings are all one organism, then we are collectively committing humanicide, worldwide. Killing is a divisive act, a symbolic expression of *us vs. them*. It is a *shiny divider*, clearly embodied by the sword of european history. *Shiny divider* is my poetic term, inspired by author/anthropologist Riane Eisler's symbol of the blade. The lyrics of "Shiny Divider" (movement 8 of *MA II*), sung by avery r. young, are meant to jolt us out of this broken record of killing each other and ourselves.

Eeye: Earth is a school. The embodiment of flesh has been the definitive focus of separation between souls that are, in actuality, connected at all times. These souls are confused by the objectification they experience, while defining themselves as human bodies. Everything appears to be separate from one's body, and yet the life inside the body is the same life inside all bodies. When that life leaves, the person is no longer there, and the body remains. Once humans collectively understand this truth, they will mature and do things they can't imagine now. Uhuru is frustrated with this as Nicole, because she has partial memory of the grand interconnection, which seems oppositional to her perceived reality at this time. What the eyes see can be deceiving. The invisible is real.

THE SHINY DIVIDER

Blood ...... is........spilling........
we.....keep...............on...walking.....that ....way.....
I...............I...know...........there's gotta be a better way...........
Our blood...............is spilling...............in Baltimore, Ferguson, Chicago, and Nepal......
What do we do y'all ....what do we do y'all ....
I want to pick up my blade.....................but then again I want to find another way...........
This...is......not a story
People live it every day............
....waiting for the bus in the morning......
........thankful to have a job for the moment.....
.....why do people just gotta be so mean........
...I want to pick up my blade........but then there's gotta be a better way

Lyrics from "Shiny Divider," Nicole Mitchell, *Mandorla Awakening II*, 2015.

A VISIBLE INVISIBLE

Nicole: In my perspective, the concept of *us vs. them* is a mind-made fictional fabrication, an unconscious agreement that keeps the human world spiraling round and round into a repetitive vamp of destruction. We keep on doing the same thing over and over and over again.

All violent human behaviors are based on the idea of separation of US from THEM the idea of OTHERNESS.

The twenty-first-century pandemic showed us that everyone in the human family is vulnerable. Sadly, a collective challenge as big as the pandemic didn't bring humanity together. Instead, the hierarchical positioning of people determined the level of devastation people experienced, and seemed to only intensify the *us vs. them* mindset in the US. That's what makes this separation so dangerous. If you're one of us, you are taught not to care much about them, the *others*.

The idea of People of Color or non-Christians being defined as *others* is a marker of white hegemony. As the US was a colony instated by europeans, all those of non-european cultures (including people who lived in the US thousands of years before colonization) were defined as *other* and placed below white folks in the hierarchy. The term "minority" is a direct example of otherness. In an effort to dissolve the mind-made fabrication of otherness, *Mandorla Awakening I* and *II* celebrate people that western society labels as *others*. The majority of players in *MA II* are "minorities" from the western viewpoint, where Blackness, non-western culture, gender balance, and gender fluidity are purposely featured.

The human family is one organism—one breathing, crying, sleeping, eating, killing lifeform full of diversity and possibility.

July 30 — 2019

Hey Deondra,

Goddess, it's been a while. From your last letter, I hope you DID get to see Ras G before he passed. I still can't get over it. Ras and his ghetto sci-fi funky Afrikan Space Program took Sun Ra to the next level. He was too young. I just don't understand. His art was so lit. I heard they making a beautiful mural for him in Leimert Park, where you took me and they had the drums and the World Stage and I bought those dolls in the kente dresses from that woman that looked like my cousin at the bookstore next to the Jamaican restaurant. Yeah, I remember. I swear, after *Black Panther* came out last year, it seems people finally got woke about Afrofuturism. It was fun to see everyone dressed in their kufis and royal threads, but in the end it was Marvel making all the cash. But yeah, it's great that people know now that Afrofuturism can open things up. But you and me been knowing that forever.

Your last letter was so serious though, damn. Out here in the sticks, you should see all the new condos they have springing up over here by the highway, lookin like Stepford Wives. We knew once they built Starbucks, it was coming. We barely holding on, working to fix things up around here. But I feel you.

You remember Baba Haki from Third World Press in Chicago? He told me a long time ago that "culture and ideas are central to our sur-vival." He said ideas are more precious than guns, diamonds, money, and sweat because new ideas are the only way we can get out of this hot mess we in. I wish I could come up with some magic idea that could flip this destructionism to re-con-structionism right now. Yaya taught me that brown hands on white paper with red ink and blue lines is a doorway to everything we need. Just write and make it so. I do still believe in art. It fuels our imaginations. I saw Rebuild trying to open up the arts for folks over in Woodlawn. Charlotta says it looks good but she didn't think it was welcoming enough yet. But they working on something, though. Better than most can say. Stony Arts Bank was an impressive move.

And yes, I agree, without a bunch of money and some big institution behind you, I do wonder sometimes, how can we do anything real right now? The way things are, and as Black women artists? I tried to get support for this arts collective idea from some of the orgs I know, but no juice. We gotta do it on our own, and we gotta start with what we have. A song and some visuals actually can heal some of this despair and wretchedness around us or give some vision of something new right now. Maybe just start with one project. I'll think on it. It does seem like humanity has hit a dead end.

It's SOOOO hot. I'm melting! My house is a sauna. And it seems dryer than a mf out where you are. I hope those Cali fires don't come back. Hugs to the kids from me. I don't see how you afford living out there. COME VISIT US!!!!

Peace!
Shareese

"Staircase Struggle," *Mandorla Awakening II*, 2015.
Musical score by Nicole Mitchell.

Struggle (Group A)

(‖: B♭ C B♮ :‖)

M-7

B♭ C B♮

E — © © © © ⁒ ⁒

⁒ ⁒ ⁒ E F G# A B C♮ (C♮)

⟶ Rit

E E♭ B :‖

1
E♭ D♭ E♮ C D♭ =‖

Groove / make end

GRATITUDE

When I was a teenager, my mother, JBM, died by suicide. An African American woman artist who felt controlled by hostile voices in her mind, she was in many ways invisible to society. She was isolated, misunderstood, unrecognized, and underappreciated for her potential offerings. Incredibly prolific, JBM continually created without reward or the possibility of her artwork being shared or valued. Similar to what community-engagement-focused Chicago artist Theaster Gates discusses about the isolation of Black American artists in the film *Black Art: In the Absence of Light*, JBM was an artist who kept ceaselessly creating alone, even with no promise of attention for her work. In the absence of exhibits and the absence of acceptance letters, she continued to paint and write fiction and poetry for years. Perhaps in a culmination of frustration, JBM chose to die, and I, who was left behind, realized that to live is a choice.

Nicole Mitchell Gantt

I decided that each act that we make as individuals in our lives is a choice that we can use to co-create our future, either positively or negatively. Each action we make has layers of symbolic meaning that have real impact on the universe.

Awareness of my positionality motivates me to understand that all my actions, especially my actions as an artist, are symbolic and layered with meaning. My individual actions are not individual because my choice in a particular moment, or how I respond to a situation, can influence future opportunities for other women, other Black folks, other People of Color, and other people in general.

I recognize that the positionality of my suburban experience as a youth in white schools had both positive and negative effects. On the one hand, I had access to a strong education (in western terms), while on the other hand, I had years of work ahead of me to recover from the demoralizing racism I experienced daily as an impressionable youth. Music offered a magical (if invisible) alternative world of endless possibilities when my physical reality was hostile and limiting—much like blues and jazz provided an alternative realm for the development of African American independent-thought, and an economic refuge for Black musicians during the Reconstruction Era. As a soul-searching young adult, I took turns that navigated me into domestic violence, single motherhood, temporary homelessness, and living on public aid. At a critical moment of hardship in my life, I was a single mom skating by with few hirable skills, no job, and few credentials to speak of. Realizing that I had to make a life for me and my child pushed me to work on my art and attain a college degree, which helped me to gradually develop more economic stability.

I write this to acknowledge the shoulders I stand on. My ancestors, living relatives, and the Black community as a whole have collectively fought and suffered so that all humans can have some of the privileges we enjoy today. Whatever my struggles have been, they have been mixed with amazing opportunities and privileges that generations of Black folks before me, and many today didn't/don't have. The work for Black liberation in this country has always been a struggle for Human Rights for everyone. Every single person in the United States has benefitted from that struggle. My ancestors, living relatives, mentors, friends, advocates, and especially my husband, Calvin, my daughter, and my grandchildren—I thank you for my voice. It is from your inspiration flooding my consciousness that I'm compelled to push these images/ideas forward.

I am thankful for the support and respect I've received for my work, and yet, I've witnessed a multitude of incredible artists who, like my mother, have been consistently undervalued. This compels me to use my voice and open doors as much as I can. In gratitude, I intend to contribute to the contemporary African American cultural legacy through my artistic work and to use art to create alternative worlds where vulnerability and equitable collaboration are crucial, positive gestures that bend uncountable waves into the ocean of our collective human consciousness.

We in the human family are all looking for some of the same things—to be valued and loved, and to make a difference in the lives of others. Can this phase of our human collective development, which causes so much global turmoil, be folded into a new con- sciousness that is more empathetic? There is still hope.

CONSTELLATION SYMPHONY

A symphony of constellations,
each moving at their own rotation,
within their own pace,
can be the vehicle to drive right through to greyness
to the other side   of the wall

(from Nicole Mitchell, *Maroon Cloud*, bandcamp, 2018.)

each

moving

at their

own

rotation

Entry 3.

It feels like the Mandorlians have a special way of communicating. Nothin I've ever seen in WU.

It's odd, but they don't talk much. They stare without blinking and gesture with body language more than speaking. Their eyes and their chests are really big too. Must be a lot of oxygen here. Can that make your chest big? They laugh and make sounds as if they hear each other's thoughts. I wonder, can they read minds? I hope they can't read my mind. NO, that wouldn't be good, in case we need to escape. There's no money here! People work but I don't know how they get paid. It seems everything they need grows, so the work they do is drawing plans and physical games and music. They say this place is pretty new. I've never seen anything like it, but for some reason the smells are familiar. The food and the air. They say they created the island from the mindlake. Mandorlians simply chose not to bring money here. Our digits have no value whatsoever. And like I said, no wi-fi, which is really frustrating, but I see now that must be key to what protects them. WU has no way to find them. They're off the grid. It's hard to know what to do with myself, not being able to text or talk to people at home. I've been told that Ma-land was actualized from WU waste. At WU we keep throwing our waste in the ocean because we don't know what else to do with it. They speak of visionary powers of blue "c." We don't know what this blue "c" is, but the story is that Lian C 2 and Accurate T found a blue "c" and transformed tons of petro-plastic that had clogged up the waters. Kisoka says that the soil here, which is blue, came from the plastic. It's the foundation of the sandshores. That sounds incredible. How is this possible? I really want to smoke some weed, but damn, they don't know what that is either.

"Chalice," *Mandorla Awakening II*, 2015. Video Still by Ulysses Jenkins.

LISTENING EMBRACE: A DIFFERENT KIND OF LISTENING

In music, listening and silence are key to the meaningfulness of sounds. In order to support voices other than our own being heard, we can make space with our active silence or listening to others. Often in music, large ensembles focus on the power of the collective sonic unit for the duration of a performance. Throughout *Mandorla Awakening II*, Black Earth Ensemble is in constant flux, shifting constellations from the entire membership (eight musicians) to smaller configurations of one, two, or three. Duos in *MA II* facilitate improvisational meetings between disparate voices: taiko and electric guitar, violin and electronics, cello and shamisen, theremin and shakuhachi. Because these meetings are improvised, each musician is empowered to express themselves with authenticity and unpredictability. The duo space allows for a type of storytelling in which

Nicole Mitchell Gantt

two contrasting musical languages are featured on equal ground—one voice is not more important than the other. As performers, the two musicians embody empathetic listening, where the combined silences and expressions of one provides appreciation for the other, and vice versa. Smaller group performances in the multi-movement suite also create a space for ensemble members not playing at a given moment to be patient listeners. As esteemed AACM elder Roscoe Mitchell says, "Silence is golden. Silence is your friend."

In situations when someone is sharing their pain, it's supportive to listen with empathy rather than minimize another's experience by comparing it with your own.

Compositionally, to embody my perspective of diversity coexistence is to make space for a multiplicity of narratives, which may not always be harmonious. In the merging of sonic worlds expressed in *Mandorla Awakening II*, everyone is not always together in the same groove. The beauty of improvisation is that it brings an edge of now, an unpredictable energy that only the present moment and circumstances can bring. Improvisation promises surprise, new discoveries, new colors, and sometimes discomfort. The actions of one smaller group may greatly contrast the actions of another smaller group to create an accepted dissonance. Pushing into dissonance with purpose is a musical expression of this concept.

In "TimeWrap" (movement 10 of *MA II*), the rhythm section percolates in an electrified ring shout for avery r. young's liberation exclamations, while the strings and flutes emerge to embed the story with their own voice, in their own time. Theirs is a dance not in accordance with the rhythm section, but one that creates sonic and rhythmic instability and discomfort.

Assimilation is dead. Multiculturalism is coexistence that commands respect for our differences and authenticity. It's a different kind of listening, not insisting that others accommodate to your viewpoints, but empathizing and understanding that you do not know what others have experienced, accepting that their narratives and experiences can enrich your life. The ability of musicians to focus on their musical task, though it rubs uncomfortably with the sounds of others, is a symbol of how we, as people, can lean into challenging situations rather than avoid them. When two or more smaller groups merge, it is critical that each musician in each smaller group be strong and focused on their role in a space where other voices, different from their own, are also strong. In life, uncomfortable situations present us with choices. We can step into the fire and stand up for what we believe, or we can empower the destructiveness we are witnessing by walking away or being silent.

Most of us continually witness microaggressions and implicit bias at play. I ask for those who know the privilege of our position to not be silent because silence allows the perpetuation of ugly "little" things. Instead, let's be courageous and stand up for others. Sometimes the hardest aspect of this is to think quickly enough on our feet to recognize the wrong that's happening in our midst, while finding a way to respond proactively. Too often I've met well-meaning people who identify as white and/or "straight" and/or male but don't recognize that they are positioned in a place of power with an incredible opportunity to use that power for good. When someone is being discriminated against, we can speak up.

Wing's electric guitar flies in wildfire resistance to the calling of strings and my flutes, which slowly wrap the rhythm section in a dampening shroud.

Too often it's the so-called underrepresented person who has to do most of the heavy lifting to educate others about ignorance or to bring people into a mutual understanding. If you witness someone being treated unfairly, don't wait for the marginalized person to have to correct a situation. You can stand up, so they don't have to always be "that person." Marginalized people are quickly labeled troublemakers when they stand up for issues relating directly to their own discrimination. For my white and/or straight and/or male friends who want to make a difference, I encourage you to use your voice in situations at work and other areas, to step into the uncomfortable and claim your transformative power, while at the same time taking up less space elsewhere so that others can be heard.

BEE wavers into a collective frenetic blues tremolo. Finally transformed into a state of unity, the entire ensemble jumps in exclamation, beckoned by young's final jubilant revelations.

No matter our ethnic background or where we are in the world, we can question our positionality and our relationship to the power dynamic of white hegemony. And if we want, we can use our agency to disempower white hegemony. It might be transformational if we all celebrate our cultural backgrounds and learn as much as we possibly can about our own history and culture before colonization and during its ongoing struggle for independent identity from white hegemony. We can only act from what we know.

Flying dreams r really recognizing mindlake. Then Liansee2's ma found an underground yoga master 4 Liansee2 study with. If it wasn 4 that safe non-satellite space Liansee2's ma had made, dont know if any of us would b here in Ma-land right now. Liansee2 n Acorately, once they found that yoga master, they energized enuf to wakn in a mindlake n develop they abilities n it. We Ma-landians r all so very thankful 4 Liansee2 n Acorately's dreamswimmn abilities. We think they waz able 2 dreamswim together as a couple 4 up 2 10 minutes a session each time n tha mindlake. It was em that found tha first blueseed, which is now Ephemera. We think it may b even more alternative realms other humans create. How can we find em? And each 1 of these realms directly linked 2 tha Sorce. Perhaps as we advance dreamswimmn we can communicate w tha other realms probably out there.

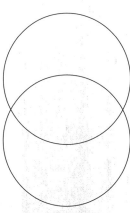

Chilren,

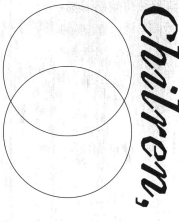

Teranthia say when our ancestors Liansee2 n Acorately was conceived, they parents was so grateful they radiated em wi immeasurable love energy. Tha Sorce blessed em at conception. N again, when Liansee2 waz born from her n2 World Union, she was so thankful. We know how hard it is 2 conceive n make a youth in WU. Liansee2's ma was a tech worker. She was an engineer. She carefully chose a sperm donor 2 make a youth. And World Union does not allow pre-mothers to choose sperm from some 1 they nu or contact with. Ha, but Liansee2's. Her engineer skills allowed her 2 communicate w an outside satellite 2 n artist man who gave her tha seed. He was from outside tha WU walls! Liansee2's dad was a poet n made visual art of a dream island. They never saw each other but once, but Liansee2's mom loved his creativity. She was so grateful to instill artmagic n they child. They child was tha best of her imaginings—science n art. Acorately's parents? They live off tha WU grid for 4 decades, but inside tha walls. Magine that! They was in tha desert when the boy born. Once Acorately was 3 years, he ask his parents 2 move back 2 WU. He said he need 2 meet someone. They saw Acorately had prophetic nature, so they obeyed. This led 2 tha meeting of those 2, Liansee2 n Acorately. Tha parents, they just naturally filled Liansee2 n Acorately with full hope n love like U all raseeve. These 2 youth did carry tha WU virus. Livn in WU you cant help that, but those duo sessions they did away from tha satellites waz fillin em up w tha Sorce energy. They literally healed in tha mindlake, though they didnt know what it was back then. They was not dreamswimmas yet, but Liansee2 started w flying dreams. She told her ma, n its a blessing her ma didn turn tha youth in 2 tha WU testing lab. Ah, thank tha Sorce!

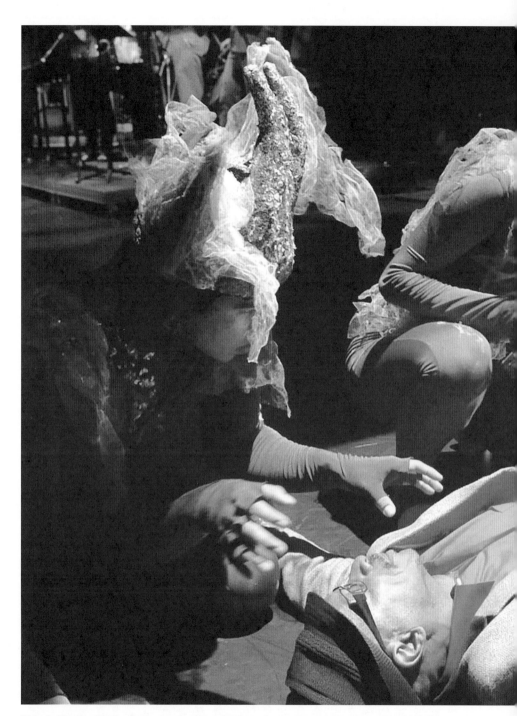

"Mon's Healing," *Mandorla Awakening 1*, 2013. Performance still. Photo by Joel Wanek.

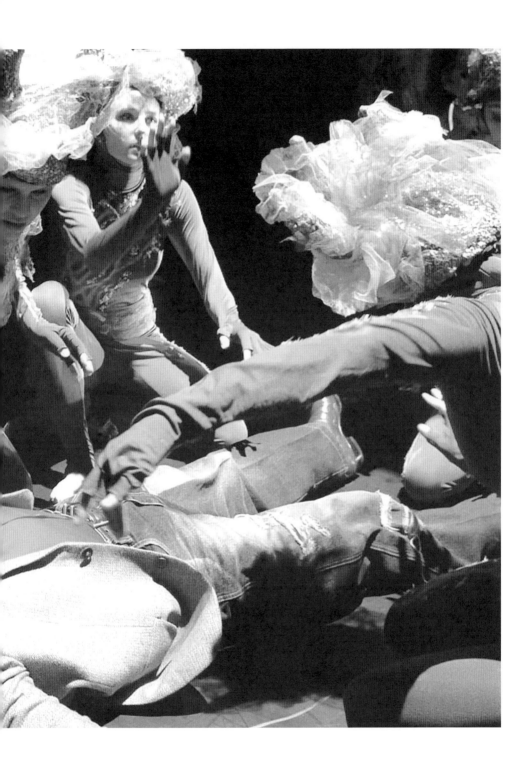

REDEFINING WHITENESS

Soon after to the global awakening and protests in response to George Floyd's and Breonna Taylor's brutal murders, I (along with friends and family) was asked on many occasions by white friends and nonprofit organizations, "What can/should we do?" Yes, it's great to support Black artists, join protests, buy from Black businesses, donate to Black nonprofits, and write letters of support for Black Lives Matter, but part of the reason why we keep on doing the same thing over and over is because

white people need to actively and collectively redefine what white identity is.

Nicole Mitchell Gantt

Race and racism are not going away, so the only way out is in. The 1960s and 2020s are comparable in the systematic inequity and violence against Black and Brown people that persists in the United States. And the global picture, which favors worldwide white hegemony, is just as ugly. If white people as a group truly slow down and look at the connection between individual identity and the collective identity of whiteness, they might experience some deep shame. Shame is good. It's a sign of life and a loving heart. white people with vibrant hearts ask, "What can we do?" and they have helped over generations as advocates, patrons, partners, and friends. But these efforts have not changed things in a substantial way because they have not changed the collective identity and goals of whiteness and white hegemony, which are institutionalized.

How can white people consciously redefine whiteness in a truly humanitarian and ecologically responsible way? It starts with claiming the identity of whiteness, rather than seeing oneself as an exception to that collective identity. There has been an ongoing collective white legacy of brutally colonizing People of Color to benefit from their physical (land and body), spiritual, and cultural resources. I know that none of my white friends want to attach themselves to that savage legacy in any way, but if no one claims it, except for the hateful ones that take pride in it, how will it change? In the movie *The Matrix*, Neo realized at some point that he and the villainous AI (Artificial Intelligence) were inseparably tied. In trying to save Zion, Neo realized that the root of AI's destructiveness was the fact that AI was the child of human destructiveness. Neo had to sacrifice himself by going within AI's system to transform and resolve it. Systems have been put in place for white people to see themselves as individuals with no power or direct obligation to those systems. Contributing to that feeling of non-obligation is the system's failure to fully support even those who are white. There are always aspects of even a white person's intersectional identity that don't completely fit white hegemonic standards. Every white friend I have has suffered in some way, which makes it easy to not completely identify with the system of white hegemony. Yet because white individuals are the intended benefactors of the white hegemonic system, white people are key to changing that system as individuals and through collective work.

If white people work to redefine collective white identity as an interdependent part (not ruler) of the Earth and the Earth's people, then humanity can move toward wholeness. This is a different thing that has never happened on a collective scale.

The more that the benefactors of white hegemony act in resistance to white hegemony and see it as a wrong that should be resolved, the less power white hegemony will hold over all of us. Here's one step in that direction. If you live in the US, and you have defined yourself as white, it can disempower white hegenomy to outwardly celebrate your heritage, whether it be Italian American, French, German American, Polish, Ashkenazi Jewish, mixed-european, and so on—whatever you know your origins to be. Speaking up and sharing your cultural origin (even if it means sharing that your family has forgotten where it comes from), will bring you closer in connection with the experiences of nonwhite people. Acknowledging that one's own ethnic group was once treated in a derogatory manner by others of a different ethnic group will hopefully help one to empathize with others being treated in a derogatory manner today. All of us have been taught the intricacies of western culture from a european colonial perspective, so a key to undoing white hegemony is to sustain an ongoing practice of learning as much as we can about African, Indigenous, LatinX, and Asian histories and cultures worldwide to balance our understanding of humanity as a whole.

Witnessing the unlawful and inhumane brutalization of people on social media has been one of the difficult aspects of the internet age. Yet, before now, affluent people and the more-protected groups were able to hide these truths from their lives. Now they're out in the open. When there is a thought-agreement of projecting guilt upon a person slain on the street—rather than seeing their killing as a reprehensible act and insisting that everyone has the right to a fair trial—that thought-agreement makes any of us, from any background, vulnerable to being slain on the street. But under the guise of other and the category of "other-ness," people believe it is only *others* who deserve such treatment.

When inhumane acts against "minorities" are generally accepted by the mainstream, those acts become normalized and eventually become practices that hurt everyone.

Additionally, while we individually process trauma inflicted on ourselves, our friends, and/or our family members because of targeted differences, sometimes it becomes difficult to maintain awareness of our collective human struggle. Part of the process of decolonizing our minds is learning to not prioritize our experiences over that of others, as in the staircase struggle where people compete over who is or was more oppressed (hierarchy of oppression). That's a competition that no one can ever win.

STAIRCASE STRUGGLE

We keep on doing the same thing over and over and over again,
and I thought,

> if maybe we could slow down
and really see it,
> we could understand ourselves a little better
and even
make a change.

Luckily,

> some of us had the fortune to stick our hands in the black
soil.

> Those that have,
> healed and can help us, because
> they instinctively
> learned that

Dark matters.

Dark matters—
that's where the mind is free.

> If we close our eyes,
> that's where we make this world,
> in the shadows of our minds.
> That's where

birds sing interlocking songs of imagination—
an image nation.

> And, yes,
> if we change the image in our Collective Mind,
> that's the key to

endless possibility.

There is a place   (in the South
somewhere, I've seen it)
of innovation,
of improvisation, of
Impossible.

Nicole Mitchell Gantt

doing

same thing

It seems impossible,
but that's just an illusion.
We can reach it—
I know some that have been there.

That's where our survival is.

That's where our survival is.

Many have dipped
to drink
its power.

We know—

Darkness is the beauty.

We have been led to believe it is not,
yet darkness is our source from which all comes alive,
from which all colors are possible.
(The blacker the berry, the sweeter the juice,
and Black don't crack.
Don't you forget:
Mama birthed us all and she'll take us out.)

and Darkness will always be.

New worlds and words can
change this illusionary one.

We just need more people to imagine together.

er and

Enter.

There's always a doorway to new ideas.
It is within our human design.

There is a maze
in the Mind.

over again,

We are in it now,
and lost!
Look around.

The Mandorla Letters

It's a battle where many artists are fighting to save us
                                        from destruction.
Lies are hammered in our brains

                    ...from childhood into adult addiction

—torturous thorns of fluorescent light.
If these thorns are not plucked with the sound of truth,

they chisel through one generation into the next of
the same womb.

                    It's a generational dis-functionality,
                              can we learn to love, y'all?

It seems the one thread we hold to pull our loved
ones dangling over the
cliff,
close to peril and poverty.

The confining walls close in quickly.
There is a timeless resistance from
death of the soul.

                              I feel it, I resist,
                              but if others suffer,
                    how can I be happy or free?

We resist.
We seek
in a fluorescent flooded little shoebox (such a small
          concept of the world)
that cannot hold any more batteries, gadgets, and
          medication.

We ask
for MUSIC!

Nicole Mitchell Gantt

I feel it,
resist,
hers suffer,
how can I
be happy
ee?

THE GRIT OF INTER-CULTURAL COLLAB-ORATION

The main requirement of most music ensembles (especially larger ones) is that each musician plays their instrument well and acts responsibly within the group. It might not matter why the musicians want to be in the ensemble, as long as they can play well. The musicians may make small talk before and after rehearsals, but whether they like each other or not is irrelevant to making good music for the concert. For most jazz groups, musicians are chosen because they play well, and the musicians agree to play a gig because they like the music and they will be paid a certain amount of money. Also in jazz, one's ability to vibe and hang out with the group, especially on tour, can be a factor in being hired for a gig. With Black Earth Ensemble, becoming a member of the group has much to do with the BEE mission.

As a Black woman instrumentalist, I've performed in other people's ensembles where I experienced the awkwardness of being the

Nicole Mitchell Gantt

only woman in a group of men. Even if the men consider themselves feminists or at least considerate, the experience can be lonely and, at times, boring. I admit that as a bandleader, I have intentionally organized groups where I've been the only woman, but with men I didn't feel dismissed or disregarded among. In recent years, the number of men bandleaders who have hired at least one woman and valued their contributions to the group has increased, but in some situations, the woman still feels like a token. Depending on the size of the group, the social dynamics improve greatly if at least two women are present. I have also been in performance situations where a derogatory racial incident has occurred, and I have had to speak with the bandleader about correcting the situation. If they didn't comply, I would choose not to participate in the project. Thankfully, in most cases, the bandleader immediately addressed the incident.

These experiences helped to clarify my vision for designing my primary compositional platform, Black Earth Ensemble. BEE's purpose has been to inspire the human spirit with thought-provoking beauty, and to celebrate contemporary Black culture and identity. As a woman-directed, gender-balanced group, it touches a range of emotional spaces rarely expressed in a "jazz" setting. A part of this mission is to do my best to treat all of the musicians in the group equitably. It is important that BEE provide a comfortable space for Black musicians to claim as their own, while also at times being inclusive of other cultures and creating music intended for all audiences. When I invite a musician to join BEE, that choice reflects the fact that I am inspired by their amazing skills as a performer, but also the belief that they can help fulfill the mission of the ensemble. Each time I put together a project, I think about what gender balance, social chemistry, and individual musical strengths a particular contingent will have. Normally, I choose the musicians early in the creation process so that I can compose the music with the talents of each improvising collaborator in mind. Each project has different musical parameters that define the personalities and instruments that will embody it. With *Mandorla Awakening II* positioned as an exploration of intercultural collaboration, I am aware that by including some cultural voices, I am by default raising questions about other voices that are missing. The project could have taken any number of directions, with a diversity of personnel and cultural languages represented; *MA II* is just one possible manifestation of the Mandorla concept in a specific place and time.

My process for choosing musicians for *MA II* reflects my concerns at the time of its inception. In 2015, we witnessed the Black Lives Matter movement raise a global awareness of ongoing

"Goddess Image (Azaziah Hubert)," *Mandorla Awakening II*, 2015. Image by Ulysses Jenkins.

anti-Black police violence, the senseless mass killings in Nepal, and sign after sign of worldwide climate collapse. My equation for BEE required intercultural collaboration, nuanced dialogues between western and non-western cultural traditions, a critical mass of Black women musicians, and an artistic expression of the BLM movement. Kojiro Umezaki and Tatsu Aoki were inaugurated as new voices to BEE for the project. They had not previously met but were both doing intriguing and compelling work at the time, which compelled me to include them. Poet and vocalist avery r. young was a longstanding inspiration, and this project was the perfect moment for me to feature him. This mission- and project-based process for selecting musicians brought together a beautiful group of people with differing life and cultural experiences to realize the *Mandorla Awakening II* project.

The social experience of *MA II* has been as rewarding as the musical experience, because we, as artists, have shared adventures together, traveling internationally and living through challenges and rewards as a group. Having a critical mass of Black artists in Black Earth Ensemble establishes Black talk on Black life as the norm, whether we're sharing jokes, cultural tropes, stories of family life, or experiences of discrimination. Non-Black BEE musicians learn to engage in discussions on white hegemony and Black life that might cause friction in an environment where Black people are a minority. Although I have not discussed this with non-Black members of BEE, my intuition says that the social climate of BEE allows for non-Black members to deepen their experience with Black culture and to increase their sensitivity to challenging issues that confront Black people. My intuition also says that this immersion into Black thought is not always comfortable. But like the music, the social environment encourages each individual to contribute their authentic voice to the conversation. BEE musicians casually share thoughts and details about their lives and learn about one another's backgrounds, whether Black, gay/straight, woman/nonbinary/man, Asian, Ashkenazi, German, French, or Asian American.

Sun Ra had a great way of looking at the diversity we have within African Diasporic culture. Ra called us "chromatic Black." Each one of us has a distinctly different way of moving through the world and defining ourselves, even within Blackness. For Tomeka Reid, being a Black woman informs everything that she chooses to do. Growing up, she says she felt like the "awkward Black girl" (in her words) because her mother didn't allow her to listen to a lot of Black music. She chose to play jazz not only because she enjoyed it sonically but also because it was an entryway to learning more about her history, and because it was relevant to her identity.[32] avery r. young discusses his identity this way:

> First & foremost, I be blk! Queer blk! Crook-id-foot-id I blk! Creative blk! Cis male gender blk! Dark & lovely blk! Uncle|Brudda|Sun blk! Nappy & happy blk! I am pretty much progressive socially & politically, be it that I have checked out on regular poliTRICKs a long time ago.[33]

Renée Baker, in discussing her identity, takes a wholly different approach:

> I've tried to maintain my individualistic identity as a musician by being transparent in all the skills acquired—skills that intentionally authenticate my journey and all I've imbibed. Truly, I identify as a globalist but because the world at large needs and supports divisions, I identify as a person of color. A defining moment of realism entered when the skills I had long honed as a classically trained musician totally enabled me to access and traverse the flip side of the coin—creativism in music.[34]

---

32   Tomeka Reid, email message to author, March 11, 2021.

33   avery r. young, email message to author, March 11, 2021.

34   Renée Baker, email message to author, March 11, 2021

Hey Deondra,

OK, I started thinking more about this arts collective and wanted to send you some thoughts. BTW, I know it's not my business, but I wanted you to know you can do better than her. I know she foine as ever but she don't treat you right! She always fussing. I'm telling you, there's a perfect mate out there for you, but you have to believe you deserve it!! You and the kids are the whole package!

Anywho, looking at how f**d up sht is, like living "the fire next time," what if we made an idealist map to focus on? If we meet these ideas with our art, maybe at least the ideas can get out there. I was thinking about the Shakespeare paradigm you had been talking about, how when people do any type of hiring, they always using some dead white man as the standard of excellence. Like if you're a great actor, of course you have to be a master of Shakespeare and talk all that renaissance sht. If you're a dancer, you better bet you ain't getting hired if you never did any ballet. If you a philosopher, you gotta know Aristotle and Plato and them. You get the picture. But what would a new paradigm be that allows each person to be recognized for the quality of what they do IN the context they do it? Do you think jazz is the only discipline where people are judged based on the excellence of Black creators?

Hmm. Something to think about.

OK, tagged you TWICE. And dance to this: https://rasgtheafrikanspaceprogram.bandcamp.com/

Peace,
Shareese

August 1 — 2019

My chile,

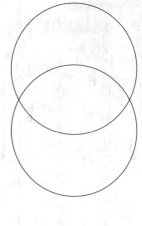

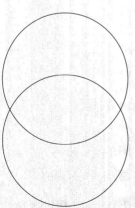

u know Ma-land, our Ephemera is protected from Egoes War and tha virus. Those without tha gifts, dont c. World Union is core 2 Ma-land. WU, World Union, is where we all came from, our origin. Tha Isle, Ma-land, is our nu world we made thru love. We collide WU with our new vision n reimagined a nu world from WU. Ma-landians humble. We recognize we surrounded by mindlake. We r immersed in tha mindlake. We depend on tha Sorce 4 survival. 4 growth. Them satellites of WU, they r so pervasive. They cage their imaginations on tha grid. They make odds slim 4 new visitors to make it here to Ma-land. My chile, u ask then how here come Mon n Dorla arrival on Ma-land shores. Itz historic. Itz confusin. How they find us here? Will more arrive? It is possible if WU chilren start learning dreamswimmn?

A MUSICAL VILLAGE OF INTER-DEPENDENCE

As humans, our immersion into western culture often creates the fallacy that we should be self-sufficient at all costs. western thought socializes us to believe that each household (whether made up of an individual or nuclear family) should not need to depend on anyone. We are taught that we should get our own house, our own car, our own lawn mower, our own flat-screen TV. If we ask others to share their things with us, we fear they will look down on us as needy. *To each his own* is a popular proverb of this western mindset. This approach puts an intense level of stress on the single individual and individual family units who must fend for themselves. The *to each his own* mindset, coupled with volatile competition, contributes to the western culture of lack. It seems there's never enough to go around, and people are pressured to do more, be more, and have

Nicole Mitchell Gantt

more, because *more* is the measure of success. Only the most successful individuals and families are valued in westernized societies, while those who are poor are unjustly treated, as though their circumstances are their fault. People work hard, living in fear of poverty, because poverty is equated with deserving disrespect and oppression. As Billie Holiday wrote and sang, "God bless the child that's got his own."

This *to each his own* thought-agreement is in striking contrast to the idea of interdependence nurtured by African societies and other non-western societies, where the unit of self-sufficiency is the entire community, the village, and sometimes even a network of villages. In African American culture and throughout the African diaspora, families have historically idealized a network that includes extended family, friends, and neighbors. A popular proverb for the Black community is *it takes a village to raise a child*. Youth growing up in Black neighborhoods know that there are aunties and uncles (literal ones and friends of the family) all around who are watching their every move and who have license to correct a child, even before their mama or baba does, if they do wrong. When my husband and I were in Mali, we witnessed neighboring villages sharing/trading their resources so that everyone could have what they needed. One village may specialize in fishing, while another village specializes in farming, then both communities shared these resources with each other. Funtunfunefu Denkyemfunefu (Siamese crocodiles) is an adinkra symbol for sharing used by the Ashanti people of Ghana; it has also been

Funtunfunefu Denkyemfunefu: adinkra
symbol for sharing, democracy, unity.

used to represent democracy and unity. The idea is that two crocodiles with the same stomach won't need to fight over food. Within a village, each person has a role in supporting the network as a whole, just as the different organs of the human body work in interdependent collaboration to sustain life.

In *Mandorla Awakening II*, BEE strives to embody and empower the non-western village concept of interdependence. The music depends on group leadership rather than individual leadership. Individual musicians share responsibility for cueing sections of the music. Another aspect of interdependence is that each individual's voice is valued. To celebrate each authentic voice (instrument/person) in the ensemble, the music is designed to breathe with the improvisational languages of the individual players, ensuring that no one instrument is more important than another. To make space for each light to shine, the music in *MA II* was conceived as a type of choreography, where the various voices do not always play simultaneously, but rather are featured in conversations between selected players at different times. This is why the truth-telling voice of avery r. young is not heard until well after the first half of the performance is over. Summoning all the power of the African American church tradition, he hits both listeners and musicians with new life and a new vibe. His experience as a master poet and spoken word artist illuminates the lyrics to transform hearts. He brings to the conversation the unapologetic REAL that our times need.

Historically, western classical music has been based on a strict hierarchy. The composer lays down the law, dictating exactly what should be played (what notes, how they should be phrased, at what volume). Second in command is the conductor, whose job is to interpret the composer's text to the musicians. Last is the musicians (the workers), who obediently strive to manifest the perfect sonic execution of the composition. This has all been done for an audience that has been instructed to listen respectfully in complete silence, with no verbal or physical response until the music is completed. Afterward, and only after the last note is played, the audience is permitted to clap politely. Over the years, in an effort to expand classical music's audience, efforts have been made to revise these standard roles. We have seen a shift in these historically hierarchical roles within western music in the twentieth and twenty-first centuries, and that shift has had everything to do with the development of jazz and the blues. This would be another book, but the impact of African American culture on American culture has been so great that aspects of popular dance, style,

Mandorla Awakening II pre-show (avery r. young and JoVia Armstrong), 2019. Image by Tatsu Aoki.

lingo, and gesture that originated in Black culture (i.e., hip-hop) are now considered a part of everyday expression in the United States. Also, few would question the global impact that African American culture has had.

Jazz, blues, and African American church music originated from the Black experience and created a music revolution, which, among many aesthetic innovations, brought communal values to music played in the United States. The archetypal band and audience roles have been transformed to be more participatory, and the composer is usually no longer the hierarchical dictator. In this new arrangement, the composer was (is) often the bandleader (conductor) who, in effect, was (is) just another musician in the band. The bandleader often garners respect from the musicians based on a combination of musical aptitude and psychological persuasiveness. At jazz and blues concerts, the audience was (is) free to dance, holler, and join in at will. This new platform led to contemporary experiences in rock, pop, hip-hop, and other musical expressions that we have today.

The most crystalized expression of nonhierarchical performance I've ever experienced was as a member of Anthony Braxton's 12+1tet, the acclaimed AACM composer's thirteen-piece creative music ensemble. His "Ghost Trance Music" (GTM) calls on each member to take agency in convening smaller contingents within the larger ensemble, deciding on particular parts to play as well as tempo, dynamic range, and entrance and exits from the score. Braxton's model for GTM is a true embodiment of communitarianism, where the total expression of a concert depends on the organized expression of small units of musicians performing as self-governing communities. While all the music materials in GTM originate from the vast repertoire of Braxton's compositions, each performance includes many beautifully unpredictable moments, created as individual musicians assume spontaneous leadership. In my experience with 12+1tet, there was always one foundational score created specifically for each performance, but the music was expanded with possibly a hundred or more secondary and tertiary parts and scores made readily available for the musicians to also include in the performance. My experience in the 12+1tet was highly inspirational; it represents a democratic embodiment of musical teamwork that completely eradicates the western concept of hierarchy within music performance.

Another luminary AACM composer, Douglas Ewart, also offers a thrilling embodiment of diversity and community collaboration with his Crepuscule project. In Crepuscule, the audience descends

Nicole Mitchell Gantt

on a park that is full of art and artmaking—puppeteering, spinning tops, capoeira, double Dutch, African dance, face painting, tai chi, brass bands, jazz groups, drum corps, and more. In what he calls an orchestra of community, Ewart brings together youth and elders of all backgrounds in a celebration of life and unity. Rather than a musical score for instrumentalists to perform, Ewart's composition in Crepuscule is a map designed for togetherness and interaction between diverse, independent expressive groups.

Mandorla Awakening II, designed to model interdependence and teamwork in its performance culture, is less hierarchical than most, but not as thoroughly democratic as Braxton's model. All the musicians in *MA II* are improvisers. They were provided a translucent (not crystal clear) map to navigate a winding hybrid score that mixes traditional and graphic notation. (One musician, upon seeing the music, jokingly mistook the score for diagrams of football plays.) All the musicians read from a full score so that they have an awareness of what all the other instruments are doing. The parts don't read measure-to-measure; instead, composed sections are separated by symbols that show placement of duo, solo, or trio improvisations. Although there are composed melodies, each musician also has time and space to express their own musical language through improvisation.

Black Earth Ensemble is extremely specialized, with handpicked musicians of unique talents. Because of this, I was nervous when circumstances arose that forced me to invite new musicians into the *Mandorla Awakening* project, testing the band's structural interdependence. However, I was happily surprised to find that these experiments with new musicians became transformative opportunities for collaborative expansion. They made me see how *MA II* was a greater template for intercultural musical collaboration than I had imagined. In one instance, an emergency prevented my appearance, and BEE played *MA II* without me. I was grateful to learn that the project worked well even without a bandleader. The teamwork embedded in the composition's design makes it flexible enough to handle varying instrumentation and personalities, all interdependent. Rather than depending on one hierarchical leader to fill the traditional conductor/bandleader role, the ensemble musicians can interdependently share responsibility for cueing each episode of the score/map.

Mandorla Awakening II concert, (Black Earth Ensemble, *left to right*: avery r. young, Kojiro Umezaki, Alex Wing, JoVia Armstrong, Tatsu Aoki, Tomeka Reid, Mazz Swift, Nicole Mitchell, Jazz em Agosto, Petra Cvelbar), Lisbon, 2019.

Entry 4.

They said it's like
a miracle that we
ended up here.
We had to have
some kind of
special focus.

The closest thing that I could think of was that time we spent in Living Mindfulness a few years ago. Mon and I had worked on our meditation there. We were there at an ashram in Bangalore before the WU absorbed its resources and shut it down. Everyone at Living Mindfulness had a nice pod to stay in, deep in the Mindfulness forest, made of eco-materials. There were gathering places and cafés but you didn't have to pay anything. Everyone did service. That's how we paid. Some ran the café, while others pulled weeds or tended to the field, cooked, or taught the children. They had developed some great healing practices there and were inviting dwellers close by to live and work on the ashram, but only if they chose to. Then WU eventually saw it as a threat, as people were finding ways to live smart, only working three hours a day and spending the rest of their time meditating and walking in the forest to make love, or meeting friends. World Union had mandated people work ten hours a day online, and those without jobs were jailed and had to work the factory and waste-compiler jobs. No one wanted that because it was much better to stay at home and be with your family. Waste compilers get cancer or some other disease working there. Can you imagine an Egoes War, a war between humans and their own invention? For what? That was how it got so bad.

August 15 — 2019

Deeeooooonnndddrreeee!!

You alive?

Hey, I'm looking into non-profits and how they all have mission statements. Don't you think it's weird that cities, states, and countries don't have a mission (except making revenue)? What are the actual goals that we end up contributing to with all that tax money they take from us?

And...what goals do you want for our collective? Let me know what you think about this.

Can art exemplify a new paradigm as a model for an alternative society?

Can we create a better world, not by running away from the ugliness, but by addressing it head-on and walking through it?

Can we build new lifegiving structures simultaneous to the disintegration of archaic destructive structures?

Maybe we can make a fictional alternative society, but we should add film to the poetry and music. We can get Ania involved. I'm sure she'd love to join us.

Peace,
Shareese

Nicole Mitchell Gantt

"Forestwall Timewalk," *Mandorla Awakening II*, Nicole Mitchell, 2015.

WHAT IS PROGRESS?

As much as we all revere technology, we need to face the truth that technological advancement (at least, the way it moves today) **fucks up** human wellness and planetary life. My brilliant friend Jamika Ajalon, who "uses a melange of interdisciplinary practice as her pen,"[35] writes,

> When we speak of futurism, the dominant definition is one of speed and technological advancement of the machine, a misogynistic, fascist machine again and again "conquering" otherness and difference.[36]

With technology as the western focus for advancement, we have marched right on into genetic modification and artificial intelligence. But I ask: Is the advancement of technology enough to measure human progress? NO! Technology, in itself, is necessary (and we love

---

35   Jamika Ajalon, email message to author, March 29, 2021.

36   Ajalon, "FAR SPACE-WISE," 419.

it). In itself, it is neutral and could be used to bring humanity into greater harmony with the planet rather than hasten our race toward destruction. The real problem is the lack of life-affirming principles motivating technology's growth.

Technology has hurriedly been focused on what nations, communities, and individuals have believed to be the ultimate measure of success: GDP.

Gross domestic product (GDP) is the total market value (cha-ching!) of all the goods and services within a country. GROSS it is, that every life (human and otherwise) is measured as a thing so that the sum of all things—individual and company income, products, trees (for products), fish, oil, silver, apples, diapers, jewelry, cars, music, gadgets, and on and on—can be compared with the sum of other nations' things. And just like in so many family games, whoever has the most wins. GROSS. This is our world's paradigm, where GDP growth is the standard for "success."

Who decides these parameters? Is the goal of an ever-expanding GDP even sustainable or logical? Why are safeguarding and valuing all life NOT considered goals? Shouldn't everyone participate in deciding the global standard for success? My anxieties about the instability of human life compel me to search for solutions and to explore them through artistic expression and music ensemble teamwork.

A NEW LIFE PARADIGM

A step away from our westernized thinking is the Earth-centered African and Indigenous thought-agreement:

All life is interconnected.

Eeye: Trees and mountains are not things. They are beings with wisdom to be shared with humanity; they have witnessed more than humans can grasp at this time, and carry the answers that they seek to many mysteries of life. Each living body has billions of cells making up a multitude of unique organs and systems that all work in concert for it to be alive. For ages scientists have only touched the surface of the body's intelligence, as it is a microcosm of the universe. And then there is the soul! We are all interconnected.

Nicole Mitchell Gantt

Nicole: One cannot separate any part of the body and expect it to work as wonderfully as it does as a whole, if at all. So why do people think we can breathe well with no green life, or survive without clean water? The western head-trip (all things are not equal) is a death wish, and we use brilliant technology to get us dead faster.

Rather than focusing on GDP (greed) and technological advancement as milestones for human progress, what if we established new goals centered on well-being?

GOALS FOR UNIVERSAL HUMAN AND PLANETARY WELL-BEING

1. Respecting the sovereignty of Indigenous people and their land.

2. Improving coexistence as a practice where we celebrate the benefits of our differences.

3. Respecting all human life and collaborating with those in need to improve quality of life for every person on the planet.

4. Minimizing suffering (human and all other biology).

5. Increasing our efficiency in cooperation with the Earth and other living beings.

6. Caring for our natural environment (enriching the soil, cleaning the waters and air, expanding preserved spaces for wildlife, etc.).

These goals come from my imaginings and can be sculpted toward greater visionary clarity with the help of the brilliant minds who improvise with this. *Mandorla Letters* is my offering toward a new, collectively developed blueprint for human progress. How do we reach our goals? Science, technology, and cultural shifts that prioritize well-being are key. The US Declaration of Independence (written mostly by slave owners) simply states that "We the People" have a right to life, liberty, and the pursuit of happiness. That sounds great, but "We" wasn't intended to include Indigenous Americans, Black folks, or any People of Color. And "life, liberty, and the pursuit of happiness" has played out to mean that people have the right to run their race and try to get theirs. Good luck, as the rules of the game are rigged.

What if our schools, churches, nonprofit organizations, government institutions, and universities made Goals for Universal Human and Planetary Well-Being their focus of research and action? First, these goals imply the need to create a new standard of collective decision-making that is not top-down, but rather central-outward. Instead of having big corporations, institutions, and governments act without considering the impact of their decisions on the most vulnerable, they would need to empower local groups and small institutions, and consult them on each decision.

1. Respecting the sovereignty of Indigenous people and their land.

There are non-westernized, less-westernized, and/or Earth-centered communities all over the world with ancient knowledge systems and whose ways of being have sustained the planet and the health of humanity for generations. Corporate greed and (neo)colonialism have been constant threats to their survival. Their input on our next phase of human experience is critical. Respecting Indigenous sovereignty would also essentially include honoring the sovereignty of Indigenous Australians, Palestinians, and the people of all so-called "Third World" countries.

2. Celebrating our diverse contributions.

Many contributions of non-western people to the development of humanity have been suppressed in order to support the myth of white hegemony. For white hegemony to be dismantled, we need to further uplift the untold and under-told his-stories and her-stories of all People of Color. An important step toward celebrating our differences is dismantling white hegemony as a thought-process and institutionalizing accountability for all acts of white hegemony. Decision-making needs to include the empowered voices of any community/individual who has felt the direct impact of those decisions. We can create new international standards of human excellence where the wisdom and innovations of every culture and gender are equally represented, with no single culture or gender dominating the new standards.

3. Improving quality of life for all people on the planet.

This can be addressed by ensuring that every person has a seat at the table when it comes to any decision that affects them. For example, Water Protectors should be major decision makers on issues of fracking. African Americans and Latinx people should be major players in decisions regarding gentrification of areas where they are the majority and/or have critical mass.

4. Minimizing suffering.

This sounds so simple to achieve, but western societies continue to fail at it. We can minimize human suffering through the development of local care-based economic systems where all humans are respected as equals and have full access to clean water, food security, quality housing, medical care, and education. The goal of minimizing suffering calls for the elimination of homelessness, human trafficking, and so much more.

5. Increasing efficiency.

Numerous nonprofit organizations are already at work researching and developing green energy, green architecture, sustainable housing, organic farming, and so on. They have trailblazed new pathways for collective humanity to walk upon. Local, national, and international communities can together ensure that human activity works in harmony with natural ecosystems and respects all living beings.

6. Caring for our environment.

While increasing our efficiency and minimizing waste and pollution points us toward better practices with our environment, we also need to undo as much human damage as we can. This means increasing practices that enrich the soil, clean the waters and air, expand wildlife preserves, and so on. A new focus of respecting Planet Earth as a living being, of which we are just a part, will help humans refocus scientific and technological efforts toward working collaboratively with Her to make life on Earth more beautiful.

These goals are nothing new. They echo the millennia-old desire of our collective human spirit to take humankind to the next level, where empathy and mutual care are central to our activity. In 1971, the Third World Gay Revolution issued a statement called "What We Want, What We Believe":

> We want a new society.... We want liberation of humanity, free food, free shelter, free clothing, free transportation, free health care, free utilities, free education, free art for all. We want a society where the needs of the people come first.[37]

---

37   Muñoz, *Cruising Utopia*, 57.

This group's language reverberates in connection with an earlier platform and program, also called "What We Want, What We Believe," issued in October 1966 by the Black Panther Party for Self Defense.[38] That ten-point plan included the following:

1.   We want freedom; we want the power to determine the destiny of our Black community.

2.   We want full employment for our people.

3.   We want an end to the robbery by the capitalists of the Black community.

4.   We want housing; we want shelter which is fit for human beings.

5.   We want an education which teaches us our true history and our role in the present-day American society.

6.   We want all Black men to be exempt from military service.

7.   Stop the murder of Black people.

8.   We want all Black men immediately released from federal, state, county, city jails, and penitentiaries.

9.   We want Black people brought to trial in a court of law, not on the street, but by a jury of their peers as specified by the constitution of the United States.

10. We want land, bread, housing, education, clothing, justice, and we want some peace.

While all of these goals are centered on human well-being (beauty and positivity), not one of them has come to fruition. We continue to endure the dystopic nature of our societies (US and otherwise), one generation after the next. These goals reflect some of humanity's moments of clarity. They emerged when a critical mass of people in the US were motivated by a mixture of frustration and hope to organize a movement for change. Unfortunately, western society absorbed and dissipated these efforts. How do we free ourselves from the pendulum of history's swing—back and forth—

---

38   Huey P. Newton and Bobby Seale, "10-Point Party Platform," Black Panther Party for Self Defense, October 15, 1966, http://www.pbs.org/hueypnewton/actions/actions_platform.html.

Nicole Mitchell Gantt

so that we can actually step out into some real change? (We keep on doing the same thing...)

PROOF: THE PEOPLE'S RIGHT TO OBTAIN OUR FREEDOM

While working on this book, I met James Badue-El, founder of a new human rights organization called PROOF: The People's Right to Obtain Our Freedom. Badue-El was in and out of prison from ages eight to twenty-one. His experience taught him that the harsh conditions inside prison might be easier to survive than the harsh conditions outside it. While trying to make an honest living, he realized that having a criminal record deprived him of many of the rights guaranteed to any other US citizen. Most former prisoners are denied employment, housing, and even the right to vote and travel. They cannot sue because the law does not protect them from these acts of discrimination. Serving time and making amends, even if a youth when convicted, often translates into a life of punishment. In essence, a criminal charge (even a misdemeanor and especially a

Nicole Mitchell Gantt

felony), can become a life sentence of jail-like conditions outside the prison walls.

Michelle Alexander, author of *The New Jim Crow*, and Ava DuVernay, director of the film *13th*, have raised international awareness of how the prison industrial complex continues the practice of slavery in the United States. While it's common knowledge that the Thirteenth Amendment legally abolished slavery in 1865, Alexander and DuVernay have raised public awareness that the Thirteenth has been continually used to justify the captivity and forced unpaid labor of American citizens. As Alexander and DuVernay show, prisoners are forced to work for pennies under harsh conditions to financially benefit multinational corporations operating private prisons. And guess who is disproportionately represented in these prisons? Black folks. Black folks are disproportionately subject to arrest, conviction, and longer jail terms and prison sentences. The US legal system has essentially empowered the continuation of slavery behind hidden walls. Too often, Black boys and girls are arrested under false or inflated charges and coerced into pleading guilty to avoid or lessen time in prison. Of course, they don't realize they are signing away their rights to fair employment and housing for the rest of their lives.

Badue-El, at age twenty-eight, uses his experience living with a criminal record to empower others, working to ensure resources and support for people re-entering society after serving time in prison. With his organization, PROOF, he hopes to unify people in the realization that together we already have the collective power to make this country equitable and to support human rights internationally. His mission is to ensure sustainable living conditions for all humans, with an emphasis on protecting the self-determined African American descendants of slaves. PROOF is one example of many organizations out there already working to re-identify our collective idea of progress and to manifest goals toward planetary well-being.

PROOF's goals are as follows:[39]

1. Enhance quality of life.

2. Enhance local economic vitality.

3. Enhance social and intergenerational equity.

4. Maintain and advance the quality of the environment.

---

39   The People's Right to Obtain Our Freedom (PROOF), November 8, 2020, https://www.facebook.com/notes/117992796781598/.

5.   Disaster resilience.

6.   Participatory engagement.

In James Badue-El, I see a brilliant, honest young man and father who focuses much more of his energy on helping others and building a better world than do most of my privileged college students. That is inspiring yet difficult to witness. It hurts to see someone with so much to offer struggling against the limitations of being Black in a racist society, just as it has been difficult for me to see my daughter and grandchildren facing challenges much like those my husband and I have had had to deal with throughout our lives. There is absolutely no way to protect them from the hostility and dangers that come with being born Black. And for James, as for so many of our Black young and gifted, there are the additional burdens/limitations that come with being an ex-felon.

What would our society be like if we didn't have prisons? Can we be courageous enough to imagine it? In working to redesign our minds and society, the question of prison abolition becomes essential, especially when we realize that prison abolition is actually a continuation of the slavery abolition movement. Slavery (forced labor of captive humans) never ended, it just changed form. Dr. Gina Dent, a professor in Feminist Studies at University of California Santa Cruz, in partnership with the Institute of the Arts and Sciences, developed a series of panel discussions uniting artists, activists, and scholars to collaborate on the idea of Visualizing Abolition. These events were in direct conversation with a 2020/2021 art exhibit called *Barring Freedom* curated by the institute's director, Dr. Rachel Nelson. *Barring Freedom*, featured diverse artists whose work was created to help audiences imagine the possibilities of life without the prison industrial complex. In a conversation about the exhibit, prison abolitionist and UC Santa Cruz professor emeritus Dr. Angela Y. Davis stated:

> Abolition urges us to think in large ways. Not to focus only on the institution of incarceration or on the police, but to ask questions about the larger societies. Why are they structured in this way? Why are police deemed absolutely necessary? Why is it so difficult for many people to imagine living in a world without prisons? And art can help us do that work of imagining what we have never experienced before and imagining what ideologically is proscribed from our imagination.[40]

---

40   "Angela Davis + Gina Dent in conversation about *Barring Freedom*" San José Museum of Art, November 18, 2020, https://www.youtube.com/watch?v=bUzuzyQZsJo.

Davis has worked tirelessly on prison reform for decades. Positive change happens only when enough of us see that change is needed. It's been made clear by the work of Davis, Alexander, DuVernay, Badue-El, and many others that prisons serve corporate greed by providing free and cheap labor at the expense of American lives, families, and futures. Professor Dent described the art in the *Barring Freedom* exhibit as "calling out for something other than what exists."[41] But our biggest obstacle, according to Davis, is that "...so much of the talent we need to address our current situation is locked up."[42]

I agree. Each of us can contribute to change by extending more opportunities and friendship to those with prison records. We can suspend further judgement and discrimination against them by acknowledging that they have already paid a high price for whatever past mistakes they have made. When we choose to see formerly incarcerated people as ourselves rather than *other*, we are supporting individuals whose families have experienced great suffering. In supporting them, we are also contributing to the well-being of the families who depend on them. We are also empowering those who have crucial insights, to help us build a more sustainable world.

Once our eyes and hearts know our true connection with others (even if their positionality is at a different location on the map of struggle), we will realize that there are ways we all experience imprisonment and freedom simultaneously. For example, our phones, as fluid monitoring systems, give us easy tools for communication and navigation, while our ownership of them signals a direct surrender of our privacy to the government. We choose not to view this as a type of "house arrest" because that would be too frightening. We are told that our loss of privacy and the increased presence of police and policing are necessary for public safety. The culture of incarceration dictates all of our lives, within and outside of prison. Because of this, in our time, no one, white or otherwise, really knows what freedom fully looks or feels like.

41   "Angela Davis + Gina Dent in conversation about *Barring Freedom.*"

42   "Angela Davis + Gina Dent in conversation about *Barring Freedom.*"

Entry 5.

It's really nice here, but I don't see how we can stay.

I know in my heart that I'm not free until everyone is free, or at least my family is free. There are so many friends and family still suffering in WU. Unless there's some way that we can heal WU from here. I just hope Mon feels better soon so we can get home. We have no idea how we got here or how to get back. No one knows. I'm so worried about my son. There's no way to call here.

"Blade," *Mandorla Awakening II*, 2015. Image by Ulysses Jenkins.

THE CHALICE AND THE BLADE

Mandorla Awakening II was partly informed by the socio-archaeological work of feminist author Riane Eisler and her book *The Chalice and the Blade: Our History, Our Future*. Eisler, in the book's introduction, addresses these concerns:

> Why do we hunt and persecute each other? Why is our world so full of man's infamous inhumanity to man—and to woman? How can human beings be so brutal to their own kind? What is it that chronically tilts us toward cruelty rather than kindness, toward war rather than peace, toward destruction rather than actualization?[43]

---

43   Riane Eisler, *The Chalice and the Blade: Our History, Our Future* (New York: Harper & Row, 1987), 13.

Nicole Mitchell Gantt

Eisler, in her research of ancient europe and the Near East, arrives at possible answers to these questions. She demonstrates that, for thousands of years, two types of societies have competed for existence:

> **Cooperative (partnership-based) societies** have been essentially insular, caring, prolifically creative, and nonviolent (symbolized by the chalice).

> **Hierarchical societies** have been aggressive, prosperous, and expansive through their practice of dominance, hegemony, and fear (symbolized by the blade or sword).

I was deeply moved by this brilliant reframing of world history through the lens of hierarchical vs. partnership lifestyles. What makes Eisler's research even more tangible are the archeological artifacts she discovered to support her theory. She found a prevalence of symbols of the chalice (bowl) in partner-based societies, and symbols of the blade (sword/knife) in hierarchical ones. I have traveled extensively throughout Italy, so while reading Eisler's book, images of the blade (or sword) in paintings at historic hotels and in museum artifacts immediately came to my mind. Watch any film about old europe, and you will be visually confronted by a multitude of blades. The chalice, highly underrepresented, goes unnoticed.

Eisler further argues that the dominance of hierarchical societies is rooted in male and female imbalance. Her research points to a historical trend that minimizes regard for feminine energy and women's critical roles in human activity, identity, and cultural development. Eisler asserts that a society's focus on the expression of violence and war (mass humanicide) is directly related to its disregard of feminine energy.

Ancient partnership societies, she writes, valued the "feminine" as the center of their religious worship, bringing honor to women and their roles. Eisler insists that humanity's most significant developments occurred when cooperative societies were empowered. As an author, human-rights attorney, and founder of the Center for Partnership Studies, Eisler has impacted the fields of economics, anthropology, history, and spirituality. Eisler is helping to improve the western thought-agreement through historical analysis of western culture's hegemonic approach, while offering new possibilities for partnership-based societies.

DIVINE MOTHER-FORCE

Eisler's *Chalice and the Blade* proves the presence and positive impact of ancient matrilineal societies. Her research points to Goddess worship that honored the sacred feminine in europe's past. Today, honoring of the Mother as a sacred energy continues in non-western religions through the celebration of Auset (Isis) goddess of Kemet (Egypt), Yemoja and Oya (Yoruba), Ala (Igbo), Shakti and Kali (Hindu), and many others. Catholic churches have had a long tradition of devotion to Mary, Jesus's mom, and some of us know that in the early european churches, there was widespread celebration of the Black Madonna (or the Black Mary), which is now mostly hidden. Multidisciplinary artist and composer Imani Uzuri has done great work in researching representations of the Black Madonna in churches throughout europe, and I look forward to witnessing her future published writings and/or interdisciplinary projects on the subject.

Nicole Mitchell Gantt

The chalice symbolizing Eisler's cooperative societies appears in video imagery for *Mandorla Awakening II*. A mother is becoming, and her belly represents the ultimate chalice, brimming with ever-changing life. All the Mandorlians celebrate this inner growing child through a "Dance of Many Hands" (movement 4 of *MA II*). The "Dance of Many Hands" video features actress Azaziah Hubert, wearing a tight dress to accentuate her full pregnancy, or bowl of life. Hubert served as a beautiful and sacred embodiment of a Black mother-becoming, as the central figure of the chalice ritual. In the chalice ritual, Samatawe, symbolizing a Goddess of life's fertile abundance, was cherished through soft, swirling hand gestures of many circling and praising her belly. I believe that the time of carrying a child within is a time of sacredness where a woman physically holds some of life's mysteries. "Dance of Many Hands" is a mother-becoming celebration, where Alex and Tomeka echo each other in a circular rhythm of guitar and cello ritual over JoVia's and Tatsu's drum-pounding dance. Phased melodic fragments play on my flute and Renée's violin jubilantly flitters.

The chalice symbol is also featured as a foundational concept for the music of "The Chalice" (movement 3 of *MA II*).

In "The Chalice," Kojiro's shakuhachi improvises a seductive mystery of lilting tones in response to floating clouds of long tones delivered by strings and flute. The delicate shimmer of JoVia's subtle bells conjures a vision of cowrie shells surrounding the West African goddess Yemoya's chalice, as the music breathes into a meditation of ecstasy and gratitude.

"Dance of Many Hands," 2015. Video image by Ulysses Jenkins.
Choreography by S. Ama Wrey. Direction/concept by Nicole Mitchell.

In that secret space, Liansee2 n Acorately played every now n then. They thought they God had somethn to do w it so they made it possible. The 2 youths developed quite a magical game. They called it "star staring." But there were no stars n daytime. Acorately n Liansee2 would spend they whole playtime (20 minutes every 9 days), staring n2 each others eyes without blinking or breathing. They said tha whole room would swirl round em. Then rings of darkness n light. They parents couldnt c fields of energy, but tha 2 together brought somethn soothing. We know it was tha Sorce that brought em gether. Tha Sorce will always find a way. That waz an important step toward Ma-land. After some months tha situation n WU didnt make it possible for em to see each other again, but then Liansee2 starting mind-talking wi Acorately. Once that happened, their connection couldnt b broken, even by WU.

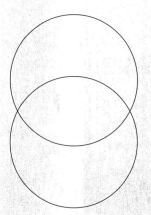

Chilren,

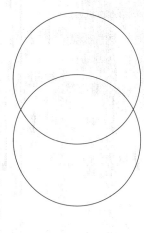

long ago, our M-land ancestors Liansee2 and Acorately created a nu medatation practice. They awakened n2 mindlake and swam! It waz they who found tha blueseed that bcame Ephemera Island n made a conscious, woke entry n2 tha mindwrap, with tha help of a few other strong minds they recruited n trained from WU years ago. Liansee2 n Acorately were gifted from much practice as youths. They began tha start of bluesoil for Ma-land. We believe they waz able bcause they contained tha 3 gifts we now know r needed 2 b a dreamswimma. They discovered tha mindlake precisely bcause tha Sorce had chosen em.

Heres what we know bout they past. They grew up livin in WU. Liansee2 n Acorately met az youths, n by chance. They happened to live near each other for a time n were compelled 2 play together. But WU did not allow mixing species at a yung age. But they parents saw a special bond between em when they met n tha Robot Forestpark. Liansee2's mom waz n engineer n she developed a secret space, a safe space w/ out govment satellite. Her mom salvaged a computer from tha1980s w no wi-fi code. Somehow, they figured out a way 4 tha chilren to connect on telescreen. Seeing em play brought tha parents joy from tha past. They parents had memories of back n tha day when folks made friends down tha street just bcause they all waz there.

DARK
MATTERS

The ideas of Riane Eisler and her symbolic concepts of the chalice and blade offer a framework for understanding the roots of this hegemonic sickness prevalent across human activity. However, as a Black artist, I found the unwrapping of western power dynamics into male vs. female, and even cooperative vs. hierarchical, without an analysis of white hegemony to be yet another trap of dualistic/binary thinking that we with western minds rarely see beyond. I sought my own way to address white hegemony as a dominant influence in hierarchical structures and its devaluing of human diversity in global culture. I agree with Eisler that western society is plagued by gender imbalances and a lack of reverence for the feminine in leadership, spirituality, and culture. In western culture, the feminine—whether in women, men, or queer folk—is usually (and incorrectly) viewed as

Nicole Mitchell Gantt

weakness. However, I don't believe that the problematic hierarchical systems Eisler exposed can be resolved by a mass refocusing on the contributions of women.

And while Eisler's feminist analysis in *The Chalice and the Blade* was groundbreaking, I was disappointed that in her attempt to reframe all of human history, she failed to touch on even the smallest examples of non-european culture, with the exception of ancient Israel. I understand that Eisler's Ashkenazi Jewish family escaped annihilation by Hitler's regime, which may have compelled her to look for the violent origins within western culture. And, to her credit, the geographical locations on which she chose to focus her socio-archaeological work represent a vast undertaking. But I see potential for Eisler and other researchers continuing her legacy to go further in acknowledging how theoretical work around hegemony (the blade) relates directly to white hegemony. Eisler's lack of analysis outside of the european context represents a significant missed opportunity to illuminate, for example, ancient cooperative cultures in Africa that celebrated the feminine, which could reinforce her theories tying matrilineal and partnership societies. In her research, Eisler also failed to address the historical roles of queer folk in either hegemonic or partnership societies. These absences pushed me to dig deeper in my own quest toward understanding human error, if only conceptually, through experimentation with my art.

While I critique Eisler's narrow focus on europeanisms, I also critique myself for being intrinsically centered on African American culture and the African diasporic experience. Each of us organically expresses our understanding of the world through the lens of culture(s) we are immersed in. Just as Eisler sees the world through the lens of a european woman, I see things through my particular Black American kinda-queer woman lens. This is a perfect example of why the comingling of differing voices, and not the blinding, narrow repetition of a single, limited voice, is so essential for establishing a wider, more inclusive understanding of the world.

If we overlap a multitude of perspectives, each speaking local truths, we can collectively construct a more complete picture of life and our world.

In my work developing *Mandorla Awakening II*, I enjoyed smashing simple binaries. My desire to collide duality is rooted in my belief that beauty, as western society dictates it, is incomplete. Western society's rigid definitions of beauty limit us from appreciating our full selves, because, in fact, no one perfectly fits the standard. Smashing/colliding duality is a playful way of destroying these limitations where something open, if messy and chaotic, remains. Perhaps this is why, as a composer, I've been drawn to musical expression that is translucent and expansive, rather than elegant and clear. I love messiness, as a sonic aesthetic, and enjoy the blur that happens between improvisation and composition.

Throughout *MA II*, I merged contrasting symbols: chalice and blade, urban and Earth-centered, electronic/electric and acoustic. The project as a whole collided contemporary and traditional improvisational languages belonging to Black American, Japanese, Middle Eastern, and european cultures. The colliding of city and rural is expressed through the interplay between various musical instruments and electric versus acoustic sounds. Electric guitar, electronics, and theremin represent the modern/urban, while the oud, shakuhachi, shamisen, taiko, and banjo represent instruments from *rural* or Earth-centered traditions. Covering both sides of the coin are the flute, violin, cello, percussion, and voice of avery r. young. I merged interactions between instruments attached to specific histories by their mere sound, and then played with those identities through the creation of new sonic contexts for those instruments. For example, the mere sound of the banjo can remind us of American rural life, while the sound of avery r. young's voice can connect listeners with the Black church, and the shakuhachi can place us in a Buddhist temple in Japan or China. To clarify interactions between Earth-centered and urban sounds, parts of the concert were originally performed completely acoustic, while others completely electric, and some were a mixture between the two.

Alex Wing operated as a wild card in this experiment of smashing dualities. As an instrumentalist, he moved fluidly among several distinctly different traditions: western and non-western, acoustic, electric, and electronic. As a white youth growing up in a mostly Black Brooklyn, Wing was steeped in African American musical approaches on electric guitar, but he also learned to play theremin and oud. The theremin is a western electronic instrument with a sonic tradition informed by opera singing. The oud is a string instrument that is of importance in Arab and African cultures; that Wing took it up is evidence of his openness to learn from and connect with others of Mediterranean heritage different from his own.

Mandorlian, Jeni Hayes-Presnall, 2013.

Since Ma-land was established, our babes depart mama n arrive woke right n2 mindwrap. From birth, organically link w Source. If born 2 Ma-land, arrived from the mama with gift 2 navigate mindwrap. Most chilren, born here can dreamswim. Each nite we have 2 strengthen tha wall through our dreamswimmn, and tha chilren make Ma-land brightest, so that WU cannot c us. Seen?

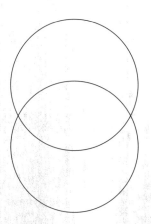

My chitren.

Teranthia say, Mon n Dorla r here cause they redy. Thats why they come toward tha Sorce. Those n WU can feel that love comin from us ova here, when they sleep. Everyone n tha multiverse whether WU or Ma-land, we all sleep in tha Sorce, even those in WU. WU iz being healed through us. We all connected. All is in tha Sorce. But change is only thru choice. Small choices, day by day. N yes, Ma-land tech can revert manwaste back toward organic state. Nothn can b reversed completely, which is y WU soil was once black n rich n oils, was transformed here 2 indigo—bluesoil. But it fertile, none less! Once tha land bottm been solidified, ah. Bless, a magnificent heat from under tha waters warmed tha ground, which bcame our Ephemera, Ma-land. Sea animals waz seduced by bluesoil. They depart from waters n find new life on land mass. Then, suddenly, insects of all kinds, shapes n colors. They came n arrived. They helped sprout young plants n trees. Blue plants, full of melanin. 4 Liansee2 n Acorately, it must have ben magnificent 2 watch tha birth of our Ma-land right before them, our ancestor dreamswimmas.

VALUING WISDOM FROM EARTH-CENTERED SOCIETIES

I have spent a lot of words slamming westernism. I acknowledge the fact that I am a complete westerner myself and that I enjoy many of its benefits. However, my point is that honoring the value of one should not diminish the value of someone or something else. Yeah, Mozart was brilliant, but so is Flying Lotus. How do we critique and define the value of a culture? Do we judge a community based on whether or not it has paved roads, wi-fi, toilet paper, and a McDonald's?

Part of the reason why isms don't change is that standards are not diversified. Prestigious institutions don't regularly

Nicole Mitchell Gantt

174

herald greatness outside of the western paradigm.

Often when a person gives applause to non-western societies or groups, they are not taken seriously by other westerners, while it is perfectly acceptable to laud the western lifestyle as "superior." The western lifestyle has seduced cultures around the globe into believing that industrialization, corporate growth, and fast food are the way to go, even though this path leads us toward a dead end. In light of the global increase in terrorism, disease, environmental catastrophe, and other devastating developments under western leadership, perhaps we westerners need to be more open-minded to the positive ways that non-western societies have done things in order to find some inspiration.

People ask me, "What do you mean by the term 'Earth-centered' societies?" I'm referring to groups of people who have lived for generations in harmony with the land they reside on, with very little waste. For these societies, cooperation with the Earth is essential to their being. In his book *Healthy at 100*, John Robbins elaborates on the lifestyles of four Earth-centered societies across the globe that exemplify a healthy lifestyle and diet: the Abkhasians of the Caucasus Mountains, the Vilcabamba of Ecuador, the Hunza of Pakistan, and the Okinawans of Japan. These communities have some of the oldest and healthiest people on the planet. It's revealing that in Robbins's search for the oldest and healthiest people, he had to find people living a non-western and, yes, Earth-centered lifestyle. Unfortunately, these locations and other remaining communities like them have gradually become inundated with tourists and contaminated by the pervasive western lifestyle.

Robbins's book provides clear evidence of how the Abkhasians, Vilcabamba, Hunza, and Okinawans enrich their natural environment. It's common knowledge that the western lifestyle depletes and poisons our planet for future generations, but it may be a surprise to westerners that the plants and soil where these Earth-centered communities live have improved through the human efforts of their successive generations. It's conceivable that the Amazon rain forest, which is currently being depleted and destroyed, was so rich in natural resources because of the positive work of the Indigenous Earth-centered people living there for hundreds or thousands of years. Indigenous Americans and Indigenous Australians were Earth-centered people before european colonizers disrupted their communities through mass murder, displacement, and westernization. The number of Earth-centered communities that remain on the planet is dwindling quickly.

Environmentalist Julia Watson showcases the sustainable architecture of Indigenous people in her book *Lo-TEK: Design by Radical Indigenism*. Her photographs and essays provide evidence of practices in Kenya, India, Bali, Peru, Mexico, and Brazil that have enriched the Earth over thousands of years. Through her work, Watson makes a case for western recognition of Radical Indigenism, a concept developed by Indigenous scholar Eva Marie Garroutte. Radical Indigenism calls on Indigenous scholars to integrate sacred traditions into their academic work, precisely because their very sacredness is central to the basis of Indigenous knowledge traditions.

A few years ago, my husband and I were truly privileged to visit a few Earth-centered villages in Mali. While visiting one of the villages, we observed a very strange, tiny porch with an extremely low ceiling. Was it a children's playhouse? We were told this was the village court. The courthouse? It was empty. Where were the people? And where was the grandiosity we usually associate with houses of law? It was explained that if two people in the village had a dispute, those two were forced to spend time in this small, crowded space until they resolved it. The ceiling was so low that no one could possibly stand up inside. We imagined a couple arguing, and every time things got heated, one or the other would probably bump their head. How humorous this serious event would become! Indeed, the rest of the community would look on in amusement, almost like it was a reality TV show. It was immediately clear to us how social ecology can shape the lives of individuals, families, and communities. This village court structure, clearly uncomfortable to reside in for any length of time, was probably a great motivator for people to solve their differences quickly. Hence no need for police, lawyers, jails, or the theater of a western-style court.

In the villages we visited in Mali, there was no sign of homelessness (unlike what we see in western cities). Everyone has a home. When a new family comes about, usually through marriage, the whole community will take a day to build them a compound. Collectively, the community works to update and maintain the structures, scheduling upkeep according to the seasons. Houses cared for in this way can last for at least fifty years, and when the need arises, they are rebuilt by the collective. It was easy to see that when everyone has a home fairly equal in value and everyone has food to eat (and the work behind this is collectively organized), this security inspires generosity, friendship, and togetherness. I share this story to show that there is much wisdom to be gained from non-western, Earth-centered cultures. In relation to the family-centeredness of Malian villages, I was moved to hear adrienne maree brown and Toshi Reagon bring these questions to their *Octavia's Parables* podcast: "What if everything in society was based on home? Who has a home? Who needs a home? Who needs heat, a roof, food to eat?"

If some western individuals today were to invent practices identical to the ancient agricultural and architectural practices of Earth-centered societies, they would be considered geniuses. Awards and grants would be bestowed upon them. On the cover of Julia Watson's *Lo-TEK* book is evidence of the seemingly impossible: a group of young women crossing a bridge grown (not built) in an intricate design requiring decades of vine growth. Such living root bridges, facilitated by the Khasi people in India, reveal the amazing possibilities of creation between humans and nature. The vine is probably happy to grow to enormous capacity, and people enjoy an aerial pathway from one side to the next. These bridges are proof that human and plant life can coexist and influence each other harmoniously.

Despite the obvious benefits of an environmentally sustainable lifestyle, western anthropologists, news media, and militaries often present Earth-based societies in a negative light because they don't conform to western standards. Again, I suggest that western parameters for defining advancement are flawed, as is the dualistic thinking that suggests there's only one way to go.

Nicole Mitchell Gantt

My children,

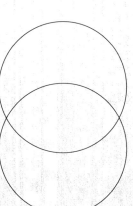

Mon n Dorla come from where we all come from. From WU. Ma-land is new but old. It was part of WU that we rebuilt from blueseed. But we studied ancient ways 2 make it. Mindlake has every memory ever lived. We found ancient ways from thousands of years. There were lands of kindness where we found solutions, models 2 make Ma-land. Mindlake showed us there were places where wisdom was cherished, not greed. Wisdom is for sharing, not ownership. Thats key.

MESSY UTOPIAS

In *Mandorla Awakening II*, the shape of the mandorla represents a shared space—the overlapping of two merging entities. I internalize this shared, almond-shaped space as a visualization of equitable collision between multiple wisdom and knowledge systems. Rather than visualizing a hierarchical staircase that places one system above the other, the Mandorla concept embodies the act of valuing wisdom and knowledge from all systems. *MA II* performances are sonic illustrations of the mandorla symbol, where colliding difference is sonically expressed and, as result of a multitude of collisions, a wide, messy spectrum of harmony and dissonance is embraced. Key to honoring the differences between musical entities (the musical expressions of each individual) was creating common spaces (whether silences or cooperative musical phrases) for these entities to express themselves in their fullness. Cooperative musical

Nicole Mitchell Gantt

phrases are represented in the together/not together concept where complementary musical lines coexist, but not in perfect rhythmic or pitch unison. It was a critical compositional challenge: to write music that didn't hinder the ability of each unique instrumental voice to shine through according to its own tradition. When composing, I often use notation software, but I worried that I had fallen into the habit of overcomposing—making music so detailed and complex it wasn't serving the full talents of the improvisers I was working with. For this project, there were musicians in BEE who really didn't feel comfortable reading western notation, which inspired me to create a hybrid musical score—a mix of symbols, western notation, and graphics intended for improvisers.

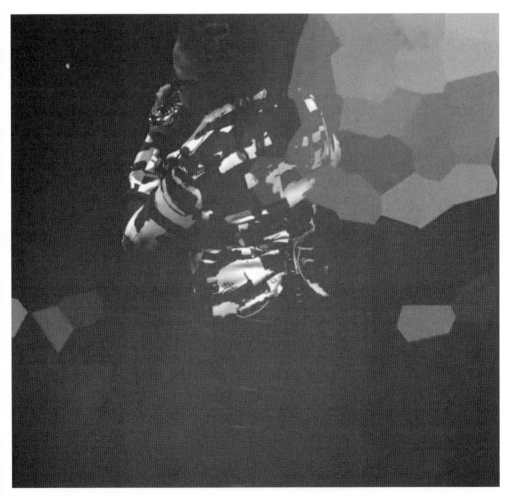

Nicole Mitchell, *Mandorla Awakening II*, 2015. Image by Tatsu Aoki.

While the collision of Earth-centered and western cultures is expressed uniquely in each of the ten movements of *MA II*, "Mandorla Island" (movement 9) is most clearly a symbolic, sonic exploration of a utopian realm. It is also the most representative of my idea of beauty. Beauty, in the way that western hegemony dictates it, is not nearly whole enough to embrace all of us, especially us *others*. In my musical development, I've reached for what I call *the edge of beauty*, venturing out into spaces where one becomes uncomfortable and unsure whether what they're experiencing is beautiful or not. I seek this edge sonically. I add my singing voice or a growl to my flute sound to make the atonal melding of textures, because I see discomfort as a doorway to new revelations—new worlds. This call for imagining an alternative reality through creative work is, in a sense, a response to the need for a wider, more inclusive celebration of beauty. José Muñoz, in *Cruising Utopia*, sought the *not yet* as a space for new futures where queerness could comfortably reside. Taking cues from German utopianist philosopher Ernst Bloch, Muñoz wrote:

> If art's limit were beauty—according to Bloch—it is simply not enough. The utopian function is enacted by a certain surplus in the work that promises a futurity, something that is not quite here.[44]

"Mandorla Island" begins as a gently lilting acoustic meditation. The voices of Ko's shakuhachi and my western flute search for each other, find partnership, and elicit distant visions of a peaceful paradise. As if the sun were rising, our flutes align in a flittering dance with the oud.

In one clear example of the beauty of colliding cultures, Alex Wing shared with me that his identity as an American Ashkenazi Jew was transformed in his quest to learn the oud. After joining the Middle East Music Ensemble (MEME) at the University of Chicago, Wing was introduced to Arabic, Turkish, Greek, and Armenian music. Through his experience in MEME, he began to empathize and identify with people he had been taught to view as *not one of us*, which dissolved his internal binary of *us vs. them*. Through music, he found new friendships and realized connections between the Jewish, Islamic, and Christian music traditions of Ottoman society. The experience helped Wing to discard his previous, discriminatory assumptions about Arab and Palestinian people. He expressed shame that his cultural upbringing included "an unquestioning loyalty to

---

44   Muñoz, *Cruising Utopia*, 7.

Israel and its myths."[45] In "Mandorla Island," Alex's oud is joined by Renée's violin, Tomeka's cello, and JoVia's small bells and cajón. Together, their musical communion gradually heats up into an ecstatic, modal frenzy, channeling intense, revelatory joy.

Music can bring a diverse team of people together to make compelling music and inspire them to embrace the power of diversity.

From the 1960s continuing into the twenty-first century, more westernized people than ever have come to recognize the merits of non-western and Earth-centered approaches in medicine, spirituality, art, movement, martial arts, and more. The health and wellness benefits of yoga and tai chi, for example, are enjoyed worldwide, and yet their origins, as non-western practices from India and Japan, are not celebrated enough. While visiting Cuba, I witnessed some hospitals offering medical treatments that combine herbal wisdom (an ancient Earth-centered practice) with western medicine. These hospitals had gardens on their grounds, both for growing these herbs and providing patients a healthy environment to get sunshine. If we examine the merits of Earth-centered and non-western societies, as well as western ones, I believe we can benefit from all. In the villages I visited in Mali, social order was maintained without police or prisons. Hmm, could western systems learn from that? western societies on the whole have failed to find active solutions to the growing environmental crisis, but it's quite possible there are helpful approaches we can learn from non-western societies. If we can equitably merge the assets of both western and non-western approaches, we can establish new paradigms for advancement, with well-being as its focus.

Part of the process toward an embrace of wisdoms from the multiplicity of cultures and systems is to lessen the volatile, competitive spirit that pervades humanity and western thought-processes and to increase mutual respect and mutual trust. The phenomenon of violent

---

45   Alex Wing, email message to author, March 11, 2021.

competitiveness between countries often causes war. It is an amplification of human hierarchical thinking and the drive to be *the one on top*. This way of thinking and behaving points to our immaturity as humans. How many positive, game-changing ideas have been stifled due to volatile competitiveness? Would electric cars have gained prominence decades ago if they benefited the oil industry? Would all buildings have solar paneling if not for big energy? Perhaps we could have solved hunger, homelessness, and the climate crisis long ago.

Colliding wisdom is one patchwork we can use to mend the mind-quilt of western thought. If the practice of volatile, hierarchical competition between individuals, companies, and countries is reduced, more people and communities could benefit from innovative collaborations. Recalibrating thought and institutional systems toward the goals of collective well-being can activate mutual inspiration, admiration, and respect between communities/countries, even between western ones. For example, what if the United States followed the lead of France and other european nations by providing university educations free of charge, rather than burdening our young people with millions of dollars of debt? What if Michigan's ingenious intergenerational collaboration centers, providing services to jointly improve the lives of children and seniors, could be offered everywhere? What if US cities, in an effort to promote clean air, embraced the bicycle culture prominent in Amsterdam and throughout Asia? What if Los Angeles improved its public transportation system? What if every city street had small markets selling delicious fresh food at a reasonable price, like in New York and Barcelona?

Hey Deondra,

Look, I know you haven't written me back yet, but oh my God, that hurricane Dorian! Mama Earth is on a rampage! I was listening to NPR and from what they're talking about it seems like this environmental stuff is going to keep getting worse and worse. Have you heard any solutions for these floods and hurricanes? Can they even stop it? Seems like every year we just keep doing the same thing. You ever think about the fact that people lived for hundreds or thousands of years getting along fine with nature? When I think about all those fires in southern California, I wonder if they hadn't cut all those orange groves for real estate and then moved all the agriculture into the middle of the desert, piping in water from Colorado, we wouldn't be having all these fires. (And the fruit would taste way better.) You can't have rain if there's nothing green to make condensation. Didn't they teach us that in elementary school? SMH. Southern California is just an irrigated desert. Anyway, I bet there's still some folks out in the "bush" who could solve some of this now. They'd know how to work with nature instead of against it.

By the way, how the kids doing? I just got a new cookbook I'm excited about. I'll send some pics on IG once I get things going good. That's one hobby I make time for even with my job. This JOB!!!!! UGG-GGGGG! I've got all this beauty outside my window and I'm chained to the desk…

BTW, do you think I should cut my hair? I wanna dye it purple and have a tight fro like Krista. She looks so dope but I don't want to copy her. Maybe I'll do blue.

Hope to hear from you soon! It's been a while. If you upset with me, please just tell me what the f** I did. Life is too short and I love you.

Peace,
Reesy

September 5 — 2019

AFRO-FUTURIST VISIONS AND OCTAVIA BUTLER

Octavia Butler is credited as an important innovator of the Afro-futurist aesthetic, helping readers of her science fiction face critical societal issues. I define Afrofuturism/Africanfuturism/Afro-Diasporic Modernism simply as the centering of Black people in creative visions of futures, in contrast with the work of non-Black futurists, who have mostly failed (until recently) to include Black possibility in their imaginings. *Afrofuturism* as a term is credited to euro-American cultural critic Mark Dery. In his 1994 article "Black to the Future," Dery argued that there was a lack of presence of forward-thinking art by Black folks. But as Sheree Renée Thomas made clear with her 2000 volume *Dark Matter: A Century of Speculative Fiction from the African Diaspora*, future-focused writing by Black authors dates at least back to W. E. B. Du Bois's 1920 short story "The Comet," and Martin Delaney's 1859 novel *Blake*. Today we recognize the visionary

Nicole Mitchell Gantt

work of Butler and artists including Sun Ra, Nnedi Okorafor, Moor Mother, Rasheedah Phillips, Ytasha Womack, Jamika Ajalon, Muhal Richard Abrams, Lisa E. Harris, Ras G, Alisha Wormsley, Ingrid LaFleur, Toshi Reagon, Ulysses Jenkins, P-Funk, Samuel Delany, and others who have placed Black creativity at the center of their futurist visions. This work has always been created; it's just that only in our present era is it getting more media and mainstream attention.

Triple Sunset, JBM, oil on canvas.

As I said earlier, I credit my mom, the self-taught artist Joan Beard Mitchell (JBM), for exposing me to Afrofuturist concepts when I was a child. Realizing endless possibilities through JBM's work and being introduced to Butler's books as a youth helped me to define my artistic vision of building alternative realms guided by intuition. JBM painted landscapes with three suns setting and Black women holding their babies while sitting on Saturn. She was an automatic writer who typed complete works as if channeling the words from another realm. Although I've had formal music training, my tendency to be ear-focused and understand my art as a manifestation of our collective consciousness was organically influenced by JBM's spiritual connection to her art.

Music has been my pathway. Creating sounds can be an improvisational practice for connecting with one's inner truth. As a young improviser, I rebelled against academic teachers who wanted me to create in imitation of other artists' musical languages. I had no problem learning to play the compositions of western european composers with expressive precision and could play solos of Hubert Laws, Herbie Mann, Charlie Parker, Eric Dolphy, and John Coltrane by ear. But I strongly resisted having my own improvisations sound like anyone but myself.

Eeye: For Uhuru, creating has been her vehicle to reconnect with the Creator. Music and its path has helped her to listen inwardly and with others, while the sonic outcome of Uhuru as Nicole will be her signature of being on the planet.

Nicole: I think that in our lives, most of us struggle with the fact that we don't have control over many things, but when we create, that intention to create has an outcome that is real and is ours. Music is an untouchable reality. It exists, but it cannot be held. Live performance, like life, cannot ever be exactly duplicated.

I know clearly that narrative is at the core of my compositional process due to JBM's influence. Whether the audience is aware or not, every piece of music I create was at first a story before it became sound. And as a musician in these dystopic times, I am compelled to express layers of thoughts and feelings through music. Channeling Black science fiction became an exciting and fruitful way to do this. Text has become more present in my work over the past decade, as I've grown increasingly unsatisfied with the idea of just making instrumental music. Sound is open to interpretation; I often need to express more—to make music anchored in clarity of intent. Because so many horrific things are going on in the world, at times I want to move away from our revered finger poppin' music (fpm), although it continues to be key to Black people's health, spirit, and survival, and I'm thankful for other artists who uphold it.

My first move to musically explore Afrofuturism was to sonically translate my experience as a reader of Octavia Butler's (might I say, heavy) book *Dawn*. The result, *Xenogenesis Suite*, premiered at New York's Vision Festival in June 2007. To cover the emotional terrain of this story, I had to stretch my compositional approach toward transposing narrative and philosophical ideas into sound. *Dawn*, in a nutshell, explores the wonder/horror of the great human contradiction: that we are so creative and yet work so avidly toward our own self-destruction. In the story, extraterrestrials have saved humanity from extinction in a nuclear apocalypse, and survivors are put to sleep onboard their spaceship. One lone Black woman is chosen to ready the others to repopulate the Earth by interbreeding with the extraterrestrials.

With its echoes of the refugee and slave experience, *Dawn* led me down a terrifying path. How could I sonify the experience of being plucked from everything one knew and then forced to dance with strange, scary, unpredictable beings? To cover this challenging terrain with my Black Earth Ensemble, I had the instrumentalists symbolize the hostile environment of the spaceship, and Minneapolis vocalist Mankwe Ndosi express both the human experience and that of the extraterrestrials. Ndosi, born to a Tanzanian father and African American mother, is one of the freest vocalists I've ever heard. Her voice glides effortlessly over a five-octave range, flitting through microrhythms with a fast vibrato that turns the blues inside out. My score minimized the use of words, and proposed universal syllables like "ah, ma, oh, eh..." that are somehow familiar to humans of any language. This syllabic focus helped Ndosi to focus her role on creating emotionally charged sounds coupled with percussive, breath-centered improvisation, resulting in a vocal score that could be simultaneously interpreted as vulnerable and horrifying.

Xenogenesis Suite: A Tribute to Octavia Butler
Nicole Mitchell

In Wonder there is beauty, and in Wonder there is power. That power can be equally beautiful and horrific as is the power of humans to be so creative and equally destructive to planet Earth and to ourselves. There is a Wonder to our intelligence to build societies, study and imitate nature through inventions, and a Wonder to our immaturity expressed in our inability hold life sacred.

1. Wonder

begins with horns and drums/percussion (and piano) sweeping intervals and explosions

Page 1 of score to *Xenogenesis Suite.*

THE MYTH-SCIENCE OF HUMANITY

The intergalactic composer Sun Ra sometimes used the term *Myth-Science* in reference to his Arkestra. Many might think that the concepts of myth and science couldn't be any further apart. If we look closer, we can see how connected they really are. Science, as we know it, can be viewed as a "modern" type of mythology—people believe in it without question because it is based on what they believe are facts. westerners have been raised from childhood to believe that reality and truth are based on scientific facts. But as our lives in the twenty-first century increasingly resemble science fiction, Octavia Butler's work seems more like a realistic guide for our now. I'd like us to ask:

Is science in itself fiction?

Nicole Mitchell Gantt

Every scientific idea starts as theory, and we make science real when we put those theories into action. Over time, these theories can change. I don't claim to be a scientist (I've been told a few times that "scientists never look like me"), but from reading between the lines of Sylvia Wynter, Julia Watson, and Marimba Ani, I do believe that crucial questions about the very nature of humanity are incomplete. We can all agree that a calculation can't be completed unless the equation has been properly set up in the first place. Well, I guess it's back to the drawing board, folks!

Earlier, I shared some of the guiding principles of Greek thought that became foundational to the european study and understanding of humans. Plato felt it necessary to establish a hierarchical binary/duality of human qualities, where emotions and intuition (so-called feminine qualities) should be suppressed and controlled by our logical sides. This concept is a theory, not a fact. And *theory* is just a fancy word for *myth*. This theory (myth) has been continuously acted on as it if were fact, which brings us to where we are today. In the western mindset, the known reality (the cold, hard facts of what is known) is considered "superior" to mystery (the immeasurable unknown); logic is considered "superior" to emotion/intuition; religion and spirituality are considered "inferior" to science. But are they, really? And do these siloed binaries need to be at odds? What if we overlap these binaries with an *and* instead of dualizing them with an *either/or*?

Darwin's *On the Origin of Species* contained racial myths about the evolution of humans. This work, along with that of David Hume, Sir Francis Galton, and other so-called scientific theorists, spread racial stereotypes in the guise of scientific fact that were used to empower white hegemony for hundreds of years.

My point is not to be anti-myth, but for us to acknowledge the practice of myth-making as an essential aspect of who we are.

HUMANS ARE STORY-BEINGS.

Sylvia Wynter describes humanity as "not only a languaging, but a storytelling species."[46] Yes, people make tools and fancy gadgets. Yes, we make calculations. Yes, we can have a powerful (and very destructive) control over our environment. But stories are essential to who we are. At the end of the day, the workings of science—all its research and resources—are translated into stories that become plans that are manifested into physical things. But everything—from our diet, to our religion, to the type of work we do, to our relationships, to the way we raise our children, to our music—is based on stories that each of us carry.

---

[46]   Wynter, *On Being Human*. See page 25, footnote 43, Juan Luis Arsuaga, *The Neanderthal's Necklace*.

Nicole Mitchell Gantt

Imagination, observation, and experience together inform our stories. We all, no matter who we are, live by our stories. To change our lives, we change our stories. Mythology is science, and science is a myth. We are story-beings.

Julia Watson, the designer and environmentalist, writes:

> Three hundred years ago, intellectuals of the [european enlightenment] constructed a mythology of technology. Influenced by a confluence of humanism, colonialism, and racism, the mythology ignored local wisdom and indigenous innovation, deeming it primitive. Guiding this was a perception of technology that feasted on the felling of forests and extraction of resources.... Today, the legacy of this mythology haunts us. Progress at the expense of the planet birthed the epoch of the Anthropocene—our current geological period characterized by the undeniable impact of humans upon the environment at the scale of the Earth.[47]

Watson's words affirm my belief that the western idea of progress, focused on technology, is a myth. While western science has positively contributed to human life in some ways, the culture of arrogance and the hierarchical stance of western scientific thought creates barriers to embracing the much-needed wisdom of Earth-centered societies. New stories are required to redefine us as people—to reimagine humanity.

---

47   Julia Watson, *Lo-TEK: Design by Radical Indigenism* (Cologne, Germany: Taschen, 2019), 17.

I believe that the idea of humans as story-makers (mythologists) should be core to our definition of who we are, accentuating the power of our imaginings.

Sylvia Wynter, in her veracious exploration of how we define humanity, suggests that the process by which europeans developed a secularized culture led by science (and not religion) was very much informed by their leadership in the vicious projects of colonialism. To justify the brutalization of other humans for the gain of wealth, divided groups of europeans were motivated to unite under a singular european identity and simultaneously distinguish themselves from those they targeted for exploitation. Monotheistic Judeo-Christian religious ideals gradually gave way to the concept of reason and the devaluing of the mystical to justify europeans' belief in their own superiority. This process of secularization became foundational to the modern western definition of being human beings. And the false rationalizations on which this change was premised—separateness and superiority—begat stories that begat theories that became cemented into fake-facts via scientific studies.

What's key to realize is that our present understanding of humanity is tainted by the historical eurocentric process by which the concept of humanity was designed. Wynter describes the problem as "the incorporation of all forms of human being into a single homogenized descriptive statement that is based on the figure of the [w]est's liberal mono humanist [human]."[48] In other words, the modern definition of human was intended to be exclusive to europeans. Melanated people (sometimes even Italians, Ashkenazi Jews, and Spaniards) were not included in that original definition. That's why, myth-science composer Sun Ra said, "Black people are not real, we're myths."[49] If we were real, he explained, we wouldn't be treated the way we are.

---

48   Wynter, *On Being Human*, 22.

49   *Space is the Place*, written by Sun Ra and Joshua Smith, directed by John Coney (1974), 85 min.

Humanity is one living organism. If we treat any and all humans on the planet equitably, respecting our diverse offerings and complementary wisdoms instead of inscribing hierarchical separation, we can be one.

Our universal human talent for storytelling/myth-making can be easily employed toward revision of human identity, and our updated story of humanity can help us manifest *collective well-being*.

With this understanding of stories, we can see how facts are established in a collaboration between our story-actions and the living planet. If we can embrace the humanities as a central study in western culture, we can look to the origin myths that informed its design and direction. Humanity, in our assumed understanding, is based on a european definition that developed in tandem with colonialism (the annihilation, rape, murder, displacement, and enslavement of people throughout the globe in europe's quest for wealth). But, as Martinican scholar Aimé Césaire stated,

> Poetic knowledge is born in the great silence of scientific knowledge.... A view of the world, yes; science affords a view of the world, but a summary and superficial view.[50]

The floods, fires, hurricanes, and ice storms that ravaged the United States throughout 2020 and 2021 were real events—facts. But these facts can also be seen as the natural consequence (climate crisis) of decades of collective abuse of the land, water, and air condoned by western science and story-myths based on GDP (Greedy Dehumanizing Power). On the flip side, poetry and the arts can illuminate possibilities that science can then manifest. Our imaginations hold answers to many of our challenges.

---

50   McKittrick, ed., *Sylvia Wynter*, 64.

Hey Reesy!!

Me again… Look at this!! I always heard about Benjamin Banneker, but did you know he wrote a letter to Thomas Jefferson, basically throwing him under the bus about slavery? Check this out. Listen to this Black man! I only included the part that will make your mouth fall open. He was talking like this in 1791—to heads of state! Damn! I found this online. https://founders.archives.gov/documents/Jefferson/01-22-02-0049

August 19, 1791
Maryland. Baltimore County. Near Ellicotts Lower Mills

…This Sir, was a time in which you clearly saw into the injustice of a State of Slavery, and in which you had just apprehensions of the horrors of its condition, it was now Sir, that your abhorrence thereof was so excited that you publicly held forth this true and invaluable doctrine, which is worth to be recorded and remember'd in all Succeeding ages. "We hold these truths to be Self evident, that all men are created equal, and that they are endowed by their creator with certain unalienable rights, that among these are life, liberty, and the pursuit of happiness."
Here Sir, was a time in which your tender feelings for your selves had engaged you thus to declare, you were then impressed with proper ideas of your great valuation of liberty and the free possession of those blessings to which you were entitled by nature; but Sir how pitiable is it to reflect, that although you were so fully convinced of the benevolence of the Father of mankind, and of his equal and impartial distribution of those rights and privileges which he had conferred upon them, that you should at the Same time counteract his mercies, in detain-

*ing by fraud and violence so numerous a part
of my brethren under. Groaning captivity and
cruel oppression, that you should at the Same
time be found guilty of that most criminal act,
which you professedly detested in others, with
respect to yourselves.*

All I can say is WOW.

Then look at Jefferson shaking in his boots—
fake as ever and ain't no promise made....

Philadelphia Aug. 30. 1791.

Sir,
*I thank you sincerely for your letter of the
19th. Instant and for the Almanac it contained. no
body wishes more than I do to see such proofs
as you exhibit, that nature has given to our black
brethren, talents equal to those of the other
colours of men, & that the appearance of a want
of them is owing merely to the degraded condition of their existence both in Africa & America.
I can add with truth that no body wishes more
ardently to see a good system commenced for
raising the condition both of their body & mind
to what it ought to be, as fast as the imbecillity
of their present existence, and other circum-
stance which cannot be neglected, will admit. I
have taken the liberty of sending your almanac
to Monsieur de Condorcet, Secretary of the
Academy of sciences at Paris, and member of
the Philanthropic society because I considered
it as a document to which your whole colour had
a right for their justification against the doubts
which have been entertained of them. I am with
great esteem, Sir, Your most obedt. humble
servt. Th. Jefferson*

Just sayin....
Deondra

BANNEKER'S GLIMMER

Benjamin Banneker might have been one of the earliest Americans to use the US Constitution to expose the ongoing contradiction between theory and practice in arguments for human rights, but who was listening?

Mathematician and astronomer Benjamin Banneker was born in 1731 Maryland as a free person, to parents who were free, and he was raised and lived as a free person throughout his life. But how free

Nicole Mitchell Gantt

could Banneker be? "Cheerfully... proud to be of the African race, of the darkest dye,"[51] he was a Black man living in a slave state during the height of American slavery. Maryland had laws in place restricting travel and citizenship for African Americans, and its anti-Black culture empowered mobs to terrorize "uppity negros." Though Banneker had a brilliant mind and yearned for opportunity to actively engage with the scientific community, he was consistently denied access to books, education, and mentorship for most of his life. In spite of these limitations, he maintained lifetime economic independence through farming his own hundred acres of land. In his middle age, Banneker earned international respect as a self-taught scientist, thanks to the support of a white Quaker family, the Ellicotts, who moved to his area, befriended him, and widened his possibilities. Today Banneker is generally known for building one of the country's first freestanding clocks, for his work with an elite scientific team to develop land surveys for construction of the White House, and for the almanacs he wrote and published every year from 1791 to 1802. These guides provided daily astronomical calculations with predictions for tides and weather patterns useful to farmers, travelers, and city planners, as well as information on medicines and medical treatments. Uniquely, his publications also featured poetry and literature by contemporary African Americans that stood as proof of the intellectual powers of Black folks of his time and as a form of counterpropaganda to the relentless and widespread anti-Black media that was used to justify slavery.

In 1791, Banneker sent an advance copy of his first almanac to Secretary of State Thomas Jefferson, at whose invitation he had helped map out the new federal capital. The almanac was sent with a 1,400-word letter by Banneker arguing for the abolition of slavery. In his letter, Banneker charged Jefferson, as a co-author of America's mission statement, to END the practice of slavery, which was brutalizing so many men (women and children) in spite of the constitution's formal claim that "all men are created equal." In the eyes of the Creator, under all circumstances, Banneker argued, Black people are equal in intelligence and value to whites. In his reply, Jefferson politely acknowledged the issue but was noncommittal. Though the correspondence would prove useful to the abolition movement, slavery based on race remained legal under the US Constitution for almost seventy-five more years.

51   Benjamin Bannker to Thomas Jefferson, paragraph 7, 19 August 1791, National Archives, https://founders.archives.gov/documents/Jefferson/01-22-02-0049.

While this is all mostly uncontested history, I see a fascinating relationship between Banneker's 1791 exchange with Jefferson and the invention of the cotton gin in 1793, and Darwin's *On the Origin of Species*, published in 1859. Slavery as an institution is believed by many to have endured because of constant mainstream racist propaganda. There was an erroneous belief, popular among white people, that europeans were intellectually superior. And this false justification for slavery is why Banneker's eloquent abolition letter and his almanacs are so interesting; they provide material proof disqualifying the racist claims of David Hume, Darwin, and others during the era of slavery. Yet, Banneker's works weren't powerful enough to sway white progressives toward ending slavery. Why, I ask, weren't the fake facts of white hegemony embedded in *On the Origin of Species*, which came almost seventy years after Banneker's eloquent letter, laughed at instead of being taken so seriously when there was so much proof of the illegitimacy of racial hierarchies? My husband, Calvin Gantt, says, "Follow the money." The invention of the cotton gin in 1793 made it too seductive to stop slavery, right when its potential for capital gain had just increased. I say all this to show how the idea of ignorance as the cause for racism is flimsy. Racism endures because wealthy people profit from it.

We all know that anything that challenged theories of inherent white racial hierarchy was suppressed because it conflicted with the (GDP) interests of southern plantation owners. Empowered by the racist ideas of Hume and Darwin, these plantation owners gained incredible wealth at the expense of human beings who were bought and abused in service to "king cotton." Most historians agree that the 1793 invention of the cotton gin—a labor-saving device that only increased demand for land and labor—was a catalyst for the largest and most brutal forced migration of Black people—not from Africa, but from the Upper South to the Deep South. If everyone back in 1791 had been walking around praising Banneker (in western winner terms) as one of America's greatest achievers, perhaps this could have strengthened the abolition movement enough to end slavery years before 1865. However, the international recognition Banneker received after his almanacs were published didn't result in his celebration back home, but in death threats that contributed to his declining health and economic struggles. At the time of his funeral, Banneker's house was said to have "mysteriously" burst into flames—an account ripe for reframing by modern historians. Banneker's story is a testament to the possibilities of the human mind even under stiflingly oppressive conditions. But where are the historians studying and illuminating his legacy? What we hear of Banneker is in two-minute Black history cartoons. What we see is his name engraved on elementary school buildings. There is still so much to learn from him.

March 13 — 2020

Oh my God.
Did you hear about Breonna Taylor?
No words.

Deondra

SPIRIT-UALITY: AN OCTAVIA BUTLER-INSPIRED EARTHSEED

Of all of Octavia Butler's provocative writings, the messages I find most relevant come from *Parable of the Sower* (1993) and *Parable of the Talents* (1998). In the *Parables*, US infrastructure disintegrates into chaos. Formerly middle-class people struggle in an incredibly violent and fragmented society—lacking family, resources, or any sense of normalcy. Sound familiar? For survival tools, Butler introduces Earthseed, the spiritual philosophy of heroine Lauren Oya Olamina, a preacher's daughter of African heritage who works resiliently with her comrades to rebuild their fracturing community.

Earthseed is symbolic of a sacred text that is (for once!) written by a woman prophet. This is inspiring, because it humorously contrasts with the idea that sacred texts across the world are assumed to have all been written by men. The idea of the messiah—a single, fatherlike, heroic figure (like in Shakespeare's stories)—globally

Nicole Mitchell Gantt

appears to us in the personas of Muhammad, Jesus, Buddha, Brahma, Krishna, Haile Selassie, and others. I'm curious, why is the Mother not as prominent as the Father as a symbol for worship? I'm sure that human-rights activist Sojourner Truth raised eyebrows in 1851 when she said,

> ...That little man in black there, he says women can't have as much rights as men, 'cause Christ wasn't a woman! Where did your Christ come from? From God and a woman. Man had nothing to do with him. [52]

All mammals and even birds and fish are born from Mama. As a woman, I question why we don't see major religions that feature the spiritual paths of women. Is it that women have personal experiences with their Creator that don't compel them to gather followers? Why is it so rare for women to have leadership roles in churches, temples, and mosques? Is it assumed that women are less spiritual than men? In my early twenties, I found some of these answers, when I went on a life-changing trip to South Dakota with a group of other young Black artists, led by muralist, sculptor, and video artist Ivan Watkins, to connect with friends of the Lakota Tribe. We enjoyed making cultural connections with one another, and as a result, our Lakota friends invited each of us to go on a vision quest—a rite of passage that has traditionally been only performed by young Lakota men. It was a great honor to be accepted into this four-year initiation that would clarify life's purpose for each of us. The first year, I was able to do the ritual. I was instructed by the Chief to do three days and nights (men typically do four) in a dark cave with no food or water. But the second year, my moon (woman's cycle) came, which stopped me from participating. Then the third year, I was pregnant, and the fourth year I was breastfeeding. My body taught me through this experience that to learn about the mysterious and intricately designed aspects of the universe, my female biology could be a key. I already had an internal rite of passage.

Multigenre artist Jamika Ajalon places Women of Color as central figures of monumental change, with her concept called FAR, or Fugitive Archetypes of Resistance. My understanding of FAR is that it names the power of our inner selves to mystically collaborate with the Creator in order to make seemingly impossible things happen.

---

52   Sojourner Truth, "Ain't I a Woman?", speech to the Women's Rights Convention, Old Stone Church (since demolished), Akron, Ohio, 1851, https://www.nps.gov/articles/sojourner-truth.htm.

According to Ajalon,

> FAR is a narrative with no fixed point, no beginning no end. The Fugitive Archetype of Resistance lives on the divide, a space occupied, transformed, and juiced by the soul energies WOC [women of color] possess; we are a transient collective symbol of the FAR.[53]

Abolitionist and Civil War hero Harriet Tubman represents a powerful embodiment of FAR; Tubman's legacy endures for generations as a time-transcending symbol of liberation. Her stunning success as the first woman undercover agent of the US government, and liberator of hundreds of enslaved people during the treacherous antebellum period, suggests her uncanny ability to transcend time, space, and dimensions.

Olamina, the visionary Earthseed author and minister of Butler's *Parables*, can also be considered a symbol of FAR, yet Butler did not design her to be a singular heroic character. Rather, Olamina was one of several in a collective struggle who was simultaneously gifted and flawed. More importantly, Butler's *Parables* offered the vision of tightly organized networks of small groups who focused on collective decision-making, not masses following a singular leader, as key to human survival. Olamina's ministering from Earthseed, based on the acceptance of change, helps her community to navigate their *Mad Max*-esque terrain and to build more sustainable ways of life through the revised thought-agreement:

> All that you touch you Change.
> All that you Change, Changes you.
> The only lasting truth is Change.
> God is Change.[54]

First, the idea of God being symbolized as transition/change, not as a man or woman up in the sky, is a radical idea. Second, this small verse entangles us into both empowerment and inevitable accountability for what happens to us and everyone and everything around us; it centers people, not as victims or responders, but as full collaborators in the collective creation of possible futures.

---

53   Ajalon, "FAR SPACE-WISE," 3.

54   Octavia Butler, *Parable of the Sower* (New York: Open Road, 1993), 1.

Nicole Mitchell Gantt

When I was an expecting mother, I experienced a special feeling of being chosen by the Creator. The journey of birthing can be wondrous, scary, and mystical. "Dance of Many Hands" (movement 4 of *MA II*) is a sonic and visual ritual of mother-becoming, a celebration of the mother's symbolic connection to the renewal that happens in all planetary life. Yet, to carry life and to birth a child is not an exceptional role. It happens everywhere and every minute, but like the sunrise, it's miraculous in every instance.

In contrast, the notion of *the chosen one* is an exceptionalist idea that we too often take for granted; it has been used for ages as a central tool for western hegemonic thought, although the idea is probably older. Like *the best west* notion, *the chosen one* concept has been the impetus for religious wars; one group believes that their religion is the best and the only true path to righteousness (and everyone else is going to hell). With God up in heaven and the devil below us in the depths of hell, humans are situated in the middle of a great hierarchy that is paralleled in the western worldview of order, whether at church, at work, in general society, or even at home (where Dad's on top, Mom's in the middle, and children are at the bottom).

The thought-agreement of *the chosen one* has globally empowered white people over nonwhite, lighter-skinned over darker-skinned, rich over poor, man over woman, and straight over queer. european colonizers justified their rampages and enslavement of African people in the name of a single, supreme God. African religions celebrated one God in many manifestations, which europeans misunderstood as forms of polytheism. Armed with Jesus, guns, and the bible, these europeans set out to "save souls from hell" while exploiting vast riches to profit their countries. *The chosen one* is believed to be chosen by God to save the masses; it's a position of *the chosen one's* ultimate power above all others that subtracts from our belief in collective human potential. It influences masses of people to seek a single leader that they believe has superhuman powers, like Neo in *The Matrix*, to save them from their problems rather than to organize collaboratively for themselves.

While the messiah concept, pervasive in western culture, alludes to the idea of one individual in supremacy over all others, we have seen that transformative change really happens when masses of people move *together/not together* (similarly but not uniformly) toward a unified goal. Perhaps the true power of *one* symbolizes the power of unity (oneness) when an organized group collectively embraces a common vision. For example, Dr. Martin Luther King Jr. is heralded as a messiah-like figurehead of the Civil Rights Movement, but that diminishes the fact that the movement was a mass of collectively organized people, not an individual, who shifted policies to make discrimination unlawful in the US. As Angela Davis states in *Freedom Is a Constant Struggle: Ferguson, Palestine, and the Foundations of a Movement*, a collective of Black women in Birmingham invited Dr. King to take on the role as the poster child for the movement after years of collective action without a male leader because they believed it was necessary to have a Black man symbolizing leadership to centralize the national movement for human rights. Unfortunately, as a result, there is little historical recognition given to these women, or to the fact that significant societal changes resulted from the power of many in Oneness, not the power of *one*.

Composer, performance artist, and vocalist Lisa E. Harris and I were deeply inspired by Butler's Earthseed concept—the idea of a fresh text inspired by inner wisdom that could guide us through our ongoing struggles. We decided to collaborate on our own music project, *EarthSeed*, sponsored by the Art Institute of Chicago and performed by Black Earth Ensemble on June 22, 2017.

For the project, Harris and I asked,

What if human beings collectively made our own "EarthSeed" text to help us reprogram our minds toward transformation out of this fractured, dystopic reality?

The process of collective creation is a mind-bending, nonhierarchical practice, where each person contributes ideas they feel strongly about, while submitting to the reality that these contributions will be altered and reshaped by the other minds within the collective. It was an amazing process to collaborate with Lisa, precisely because writing poetry and creating music are intimate spaces that have been my personal refuge for complete freedom. In a world that is not kind, in which acceptance and love are not plentiful, music and poetry can provide an alternative realm where we can safely be our full selves without criticism or danger. It was a beautiful unfolding to learn that I could share this sacred space with another person and

Nicole Mitchell Gantt

not feel limited or uncomfortable in any way. Neither of us claims sections of the work, but rather we both claim all of the work as our collective creation, *EarthSeed*. Hopefully, Octavia is proud. In 2020, FPE Records released a live recording of the premiere of *EarthSeed*, performed by BEE, on Octavia's birthday, June 22.

March 30 — 2020

Hey Reesy,

It's been FOREVER since I wrote you. I Marco Polo-ed you but you haven't answered so hopefully you see this. Things are so crazy right now. Sorry I was so out of touch. It's too much to carry right now, between Breonna's murder and this virus. Your family doing OK? My fam is hanging on. So, to take things off my mind....

First of all B, get off my boo. She's amazing, OK? I've never been this happy and you know that. We made up and all is cool so stop worrying. I just get jealous when the kids act like they love her more than me and that was getting on my nerves, but it wasn't even her fault and it's not a big deal. Just a miscommunication. Besides, you don't hear me giving you problems about Tadique—and we KNOW he ain't perfect. None of us are. I know you protective but sometimes it comes off overbearing.

Second, stop complaining! At least you HAVE a job!!!! I hope you're doing OK out there. I was reading our last emails and yes, this climate crisis is EPIC.

Third, you need to get it in your gorgeous nappy head that Black women ARE the answer right now, OK?! I mean, look at Octavia, it's really starting to feel like we are living inside one of her novels. Talk about prophecy. We have to stick together.

And fourth, life is too short. I just barely got out of Nola before this whole virus thing all went down. I think they might ground all of us with this virus. It's surreal that this thing is worldwide. And thank goodness, my landlord will let us stay with cheaper rent until this is over. All my gigs are cancelled through September, but we'll find a way. I know I'm blessed, so I try to stay positive.

I was thinking, we really should get this arts collective you were talking about off the ground. Now might be the perfect time. Hit me up about

Nicole Mitchell Gantt

it. I have to stop with IG and FB. The trauma is too overwhelming, so reach out here.

AND, like I said, Octavia's *Parables* are literally about right now. It's haunting how close it is to our moment. The other night I re-read *Kindred*, and my ass was up all night. I couldn't put it down. That story blows my mind. I'm wondering if *Kindred* was the first book to deal with time travel and slavery. Honestly, I think Harriet Tubman really did move through portholes that folded space and time. That was so brilliant how Ta-Nehisi Coates positioned Harriet that way in *The Water Dancer*. Harriet had that divine connection.

You heard about Moor Mother and Rasheedah Phillips in Philly? They actually created a way of life called Black Quantum Futurism that helps us jump portholes and decolonize our minds from the hamster wheel of the western clock we are all running on. Now they doin sh*t! They have a publishing house and an organization and everything.

Hey. Make sure you are where you want to be with who you want to be with before they do this lockdown thing. It's getting ready to be like the old South Africa, with us carrying passes and sh*t. It ain't new to us, but the fact that the whole world is doing it is deep. I can't think about my babies being so far when they with their dad, but they said we can keep up our custody schedule even with the virus. I'm sure it's crazy where you are too, yes? Me and the Esty are good. It's just that we're separated in two different places during this containment now. I try not to think much about it. I wonder how long this sh*t is going to last.

I'm gonna go take a ride to the beach while I still can.

I'll holla,
Deondra.

Time can be drawn,

chilren. For us its a circle. For WU its a line. We can enter doorways thru the mindlake. Thats how we talk to Acorately. ah, bless.

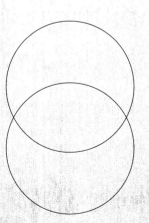

The Mandorla Letters

Tomeka Reid and Mazz Swift, *Mandorla Awakening II*, 2015. Image by Tatsu Aoki.

TIMEWRAP

Back when the days are too long and the sweat pours endlessly, on the fields of cotton, and the streets of the city, picking strawberries and caning sugar or even laying down the tracks of the rail. Where we build bridges.

A moan.........emerged. That moan was
a seed of liberation. That moan is love for life. That moan is determination. That moan has been the grain of sand that calls our destiny and survival of humanity.

A small and seemingly simple sound wavers between the known and unknown, light and darkness.
The love and hate.

That moan is a small kernel of life.
Where we dip our minds into the bright.
We develop a new territory where we'll reside.
Where we dip our minds into the bright.

Where the velvet blanket of coal black night
covered the sky with piercings of light
from the other side.

We develop a new territory where we'll reside.
Where the velvet blanket of coal black night
covered the sky with piercings of light
from the other side.

April 7 – 2020

Hey Deondra Love,

Thanks for writing back. OK......I hear you. Esty's cool. I'm in full support. It's just that you move so fast in these relationships, Queen. I just couldn't respond about Breonna. I'm so angry I can't see straight. They HAVE to give her justice. How is it OK to kill someone in their sleep? What happened to fair trial? It's the same way they killed Fred Hampton in Chicago. How is that OK? It's NOT OK! We have to keep posting about it until those cops are put in jail.

And this virus—Mama Earth is really telling us to f*** off! I wish after all these thousands of years of dreaming separatism and greed and patriarchy, I wish we could wake up one sunny morning to cling to each other's differences like hydrogen and oxygen and the Orisha. See? I still got some imagination. I do have some ideas for our collective. I'll send you some examples of projects we can work on together.

Thanks for sending me your fiction ideas. It really helps to read that right now. Gives me hope. I want to see this utopian island you're imagining. You remember way back when we first met? I just wanna say I appreciate you, sis. You've been with me through a lot of changes. Good changes. Actually, we've always had some visions in common. Life is too short.

Check this stuff out below that I sent and let me know if any of my process for this project below could be used as a starting point for what we are trying to do. The work would be even better if it was not just between us but if it could be something that lots of people could try in their own way. But that takes skills. We gotta start small. You know, the way adrienne maree brown speaks of the cumulative power of small positive actions in *Emergent Strategy*. I love her. Her new book, *Pleasure Activism*, is so real! I wanna be out and free like that. That's why I wrote this thing you're reading now. I visualize all of us collaborating on new paths of understanding and building new ways of doing things that can replace the destructive habits we participate in. Like in Octavia's *Parable of the Talents*. All this has got me thinking about a lot of underlying stuff we take for granted.

I'm hoping that the music and these thoughts can maybe spark a few new ideas. If people are inspired to break out of this pattern of doing the same thing on and on, that would be amazing.

Hey, I tried the coffee enema you were talking about. Great feeling, but you say do this every week? That seems a bit much.

Air hugs,
Shareese

A "SEED" SPRING- BOARD FOR ALTERNATIVE REALITIES

My experience as a member of the Association for the Advance-ment of Creative Musicians showed me how powerful one idea can be when embraced by a whole group of people. In 1965, on Chica-go's South Side, four African American musicians—Muhal Richard Abrams, Phil Cohran, Jodie Christian, and Steve McCall—had the idea to establish an organization that would come to exemplify the endless possibilities of Black creativity. Not limited by popular thought-agreements, musicians of the AACM created a new narrative

Nicole Mitchell Gantt

for Black people, especially in Chicago—one that placed Black artists at the center of cultural innovation and experimentalism in twentieth- and twenty-first-century music. Members of the AACM have created a new paradigm for arts collectives. The idea of collectively supporting each individual's discovery and expression of their own singular voice, rather than imposing rules for artistic expression, is a unique and empowering concept for a group. Members support one another by embracing their diversity; we share resources in the spirit of interdependence. We share in the belief that there is enough (an abundance of blessings) for all to succeed. From its inception, the AACM claimed agency in using art and imagination toward collective support of individual contributions of new compositional approaches and improvisational languages to the field of music. Among the many incredibly unique artists to have emerged from this seed are JoVia Armstrong, Renée Baker, Anthony Braxton, Coco Elysses, Ben Lamar, George E. Lewis, Amina Claudine Meyers, Roscoe Mitchell, Mankwe Ndosi, Avreeayl Ra, Mike Reed, Tomeka Reid, and Henry Threadgill. What is most inspiring to me about the AACM is the power of its seed idea, embodied in the longtime leadership of Muhal Richard Abrams: make original music. Something so direct and elegantly simple has triggered an abundance of creativity over generations. In observing the power of this one idea, this seed, I recognize the power that we have as people to reshape our future, if we think and act collectively.

In my ruminations on the power of seeds to both be whole and yet to unfold into completeness, I often think about the roots of the blues. I see the blues as not just music but as a core essence of Black culture in the United States: a spirit of resilience that can never be crushed. Examining the blues more closely, I get down to a moan. A melodious moan could express Black anguish and pain but also vitality and tenacity. During slavery, perhaps it was the wordless moan, the core sound of the blues, that communicated hope and togetherness to others who worked in what Ta-Nehisi Coates calls the Task. While tasking, a wordless, emotive, spirit-infused moan could say what the colonizers' English language could not, or what was forbidden to utter. In "Timewrap," the last movement of *Mandorla Awakening II*, avery r. young sings about the power of the moan in a jubilation of Black resilience and hope. I purposely shift from past to present to future in the movement to echo the reverberation of the struggle across time, while BEE jumps in with a dance groove of rhythmical repetition and where Alex Wing's electric guitar shouts blue amens in response to avery's jubilation.

April 30 — 2020

Wow, Reesy!

Sorry it took me so long again. (You know how it is.)

Still no justice yet. I've been so scared. My son has been going out there to protest. But I'm proud of him at the same time. Let's change the subject.

Hey, did you finish re-reading Octavia's *Xenogenesis* Trilogy yet? I was thinking about the Oolois. You know, those strange, disgusting space creatures that Lilith was forced to connect with? Octavia describes them as being seductive, even though they are horrifying. But somehow they seem almost comical, and yet possibly deadly. But the main thing I was wondering about is, you know, how we say Octavia is so prophetic? What if the Ooloi, with all their tentacles (like an octopus), are actually here now and we just haven't known it? Think about it. The Ooloi is the mediator between humans having sex, right? Like two people can't connect directly but have to both connect to the same Ooloi as their third partner, right? Well, now that we're all stuck online with no contact, what if the Ooloi was the screen! Since they shut us down, the only way we can connect with each other is through screens. Screens fold spaces, fold geographies into one place. And all those screens everywhere could be the many arms of the Ooloi, basically controlling us, yet offering us the only way we can be together. Yikes! What do you think?

Anyway, YES. When I was looking at your drafts I got an idea. Let's weave both our pieces together like a quilt and see how it turns out. I've got the creative nonfiction going on and you can transition your fiction in between. What do you think? I'll add some of my thoughts into your philosophical parts, and you can add some of your ideas into my fiction part.

YES! We need to hurry though because we don't know how long books are going to last! Maybe we should just post it online? This stay-at-home order is the most! We should have come to visit you when we could. Damn.

All things good,
Deondra

Interstellar Mothers, JBM, oil on canvas, 1977.

IDEAS TO SUPPORT HUMAN HAPPINESS

What are the key principles that can help us to build anW equitable Earth-centered world?

This question led me to ruminate on nine interconnected principles that we encounter in our daily lives. If we value them all, perhaps we can move toward greater collective happiness and well-being. They are listed here in no particular order.

Nicole Mitchell Gantt

1. Oneness.

Human beings aside, all other life forms on planet Earth collaborate in ecological balance. Let's join them! A global cultural shift away from narcissism and toward the belief that each and every life form (human and otherwise) is miraculous and of precious value can restabilize humanity and the Earth. All people desire to feel belonging, to be appreciated, and to do something meaningful in our lives. As more of us recognize and embrace Oneness with all other life on the planet, we can better organize collective efforts toward collective human wellness in cooperation with the Earth.

2. Love.

We all seek love and relationships with others. If we honor this collective desire, we can increase our empathy toward understanding that all humans are part of one organism: humanity. We can grasp that "hurting an other hurts our selves and hurting our selves hurts others," to quote from the Harris/Mitchell *EarthSeed*. Relationships of love include our personal relationships as well as our relations with the Earth (with land, animals, plants, insects, etc.). Loving unconditionally is work. It takes courage to be honest and speak up at times when it is easier to be silent or walk away. Perhaps truest love is when we can be 100% honest with each other at all times without fear. But other, not-so-pretty relationships are where our lovework is most needed and where we have the most potential for growth. Like microcosms, personal relationships impact greater communities, cultures, and societies, so this work is essential. Loving might mean pushing back in one moment and listening in another. Loving can definitely be uncomfortable, and yet that discomfort is the tension that brings growth. It is work to learn how to love ourselves and others.

3. Abundance.

When we look to nature, we see its abundance. One fruit-bearing tree can grow more fruit than any one person or even one family can eat. When the fruit is plucked, many more grow back in its place. My husband grew a small vegetable garden in front of our house, and no matter how many greens we cut and gave away, they just kept coming back. Among mammals, the output of a mothers' milk naturally increases as her baby grows. The planet has enough resources to sustain all life, but it is our responsibility as humans to manage these resources and minimize our waste, while respecting the Earth and other life-forms. We can learn from how nonindustrial, non-western, Earth-centered societies have proven over thousands of years that it's possible to develop communities that are environmentally sustainable.

4. Vulnerability.

As individuals and members of the human species, we are dependent on one another and Mama Earth. We are vulnerable to one another, even for our very breath: the plant-network (the Earth's foundation of soil, plants, and air) provides us the oxygen we need, while we as mammals provide plants with carbon dioxide. All of life is mutually interdependent. If we know this to be true, why would we hurt one another? If we can reframe our thinking based on this awareness, I believe we can achieve balance and happiness. If we can recognize Mama Earth as a part of us, and ourselves as a small part of Her, we will experience greater joy and wisdom.

5. Diversity.

Diversity is an asset. Diversity is an expressive aspect of Mama Earth's abundance. A tiger in China looks different from a tiger in India and different from one in Malaysia. Even with their differences, they are all tigers, and they are all magnificent. We want to honor a red poppy for its unique qualities—it is unlike any other flower, yet just as wonderful as any flower. If we can reach to appreciate differences in culture, race, gender, beliefs, and abilities in this same way, we'll be much closer to Oneness. We, as humans, are in an adolescent stage of maturity. We judge and impose suffering on others based on physical and ideological differences. If we look, we find that diversity in nature contributes to the resilience of all life-forms. People exemplify a diverse range of experiences, cultural backgrounds, philosophies, and physical attributes. Yet people fear these differences. The more we are able to respect and recognize differences as assets in human relationships, the closer we are to reaching a place of equity. Simply said, if we can accept another person and treat them as a beloved family member, we will advance the maturity of humanity.

6. Imagination.

Imagination is our greatest resource as humans. If we use it to visualize new ways and new worlds, we can contribute to the creation of a wondrous future. Collectively and individually, we can use our imaginations to solve any problem, duplicate anything in existence, or create something never seen before.

7. Agency.

We, as people, have agency to act, move, and create. Even as individuals, we have the power to collaborate with the universe in the formation of our future through the focused intent of our thoughts and actions.

8. Art.

Art is intrinsically human. Art has the power to transform. Art can raise questions. It can inspire new perspectives on life and empower us to do things differently. Art can also facilitate invention across a wide spectrum, from architecture to technology to human relations and beyond. And with greater collaboration between art and the sciences, the possibilities are endless.

9. Institutions.

Institutions are organized networks of people who make things happen. I think of them as networks of family bands. Our families, if consciously worked on, can be institutions of great positive impact. As we redesign our western thought-agreements and expand our consciousness toward universal well-being, new, generative institutions will emerge, while the older, more destructive ones will eventually lose support.

It brings me some hope to know that there are people and institutions all over the world using their agency, imagination, and love to achieve greater happiness and well-being. I see this work manifested in all kinds of ways. My husband has been gardening, transforming the lawn into an abundance of organic food, and sharing inspiration through podcasts. Others do this work by simply driving someone to the store in exchange for groceries. Still others may give encouragement to someone with a great idea that needs confidence to see it through.

Costa Rica has been making significant governmental efforts to top the Happiness Index and improve quality of life for its citizens.[55] According to Josephine Moulds in her 2019 article for the World Economic Forum, Costa Rica demilitarized in 1948, and since then has increased its investment in education and healthcare for its people, no matter their economic status. It has invested significantly in reforestation projects to combat climate change and improve air quality, and more than 99% of its electricity comes from renewable sources.[56]

In 2008, Senegal established a national agency to sponsor the creation of 14,000 ecovillages.[57] This was the result of a grassroots movement of people working to undo poverty and desertification in their respective villages. Under government sponsorship, future models were developed for rural Senegal to establish self-sufficiency for food, water, electricity, and wood. This is just one example of how local communities can work together toward a better collective future.

In 2018, the nations of Scotland, Iceland, and New Zealand established the Wellbeing Economy Alliance (WEAll) to collaborate on redesigning economic policy. In a TED Talk, Nicola Sturgeon, Scotland's first woman prime minister, explained that "the goal of economic policy should be well-being—how happy a population is, not just how wealthy a population is." Together with the leaders of Iceland and New Zealand (all women leaders—just sayin'), she is working to decrease carbon emissions, correct economic inequalities, and increase access to good housing and green spaces.[58]

55   Lindsay Fendt, "Why Costa Rica Is One of the Happiest Countries in the World," *The Huffington Post*, September 6, 2018, https://www.huffpost.com/entry/costa-rica-happiness-well-being_n_5b6184a8e4b0de86f49c7611.

56   Josephine Moulds, "Costa Rica is one of the world's happiest countries. Here's what it does differently," World Economic Forum, January 31, 2019, https://www.weforum.org/agenda/2019/01/sun-sea-and-stable-democracy-what-s-the-secret-to-costa-rica-s-success/.

57   Erika Alatalo, "Senegalese villages fight desertification and poverty by becoming ecovillages," Field Study of the World, August 19, 2018, https://www.fieldstudyoftheworld.com/senegalese-villages-fight-desertification-poverty-becoming-ecovillages/.

58   Nicola Sturgeon, "Why governments should prioritize well-being," TED Talk, July 29, 2019, https://www.youtube.com/watch?v=gJzSWacrkKo&t=1s.

Anna Chrysopoulou, an advocacy coordinator of the Wellbeing Economy Alliance, lists the following as core principles to a wellbeing economy:[59]

1. Restoring a harmonious relationship between society and nature.

2. Ensuring a fair distribution of resources to address economic inequality.

3. Supporting healthy and resilient individuals and communities.

I see the enormous potential of the WEAll, yet I respectfully encourage greater recognition of similar and earlier efforts by non-western governments. Couldn't Costa Rica be a member of the WEAll? Can Senegal's efforts be acknowledged? How can we ensure that this conceptually beautiful economic design will not be poisoned by white hegemony? We've seen how the US Constitution has played out. That "all men are created equal" are just words, that "all" doesn't mean everyone. I sincerely hope that these new efforts do not ignore or perpetuate the damage of racial disparities endemic to white hierarchical thinking.

---

59   Anna Chrysopoulou, "The Vision of a Well-Being Economy," *Stanford Social Innovation Review*, December 16, 2020, https://ssir.org/articles/entry/the_vision_of_a_well_being_economy.

Entry 6.

Mon is better!
He's awake! It
was a fast
recovery.
Perhaps that's
why we are here!

He told me so many things! He was in the mindlake and he saw the dreamswimmas! He says he met Acorately and he understands some of what these Mandorlians have been telling us. That's amazing. I don't get it, but I'm thankful he's all right. Now that we've relaxed a bit, I'm starting to get annoyed and want to go home. This mindwrap stuff is too intense for me. The food is getting to me too. A burger would be good about now. But Mon wants to learn more. I hope he doesn't want to stay. At WU we were accustomed to privacy. Especially in our thoughts. But there's none here. They can hear me right now! We don't know what they are thinking, but now we know for sure they know what we're thinking. They've been sing-talking out loud this whole time just for our benefit! And they laugh at us all the time! I feel naked. It's scary not having space. Thought space. Mind space. They tell us ugliness swarms and festers there in our thoughts. The Mandorlians believe that it was separatism and privacy in WU that led to the me-first thinking and eventually the Egoes Wars. They know everything about our life in WU but we don't hardly know nothing about them. They say because we don't wake in the mindwrap our imaginations feed WU and the Egoes Wars.

They say our imaginations are captive to the screens we watch.

232

I don't fully understand. It seems that in the Ma-land mindwrap, every living being can feel the thoughts and feelings of all other beings. Maybe they are all empaths and can hear the collective thoughts of all, like a sea of voices. Maybe that's what the blue is. They told us that if we don't have proper training, and if we wake in the mindwrap, we could go mad hearing all those voices and lose ourselves. Sounds scary, like maybe what my sister was hearing before she disappeared. But yet, maybe we're already part of the mindwrap just being here? Proximity means something too. I think our thoughts are synced with theirs because we're here on the island. If we wake in the mindlake with untrained thoughts, they say our negativity can damage everyone and disrupt the whole island. They say it's taking a lot of tech energy to keep us here untrained while they protect the health of the island. Ma-land re-creates itself gradually every twenty-one days through the meditative thoughts of Mandorlians in the mindwrap. We somehow found our way to these shores even though we were not awake in the mindwrap. This mindwrap is key to the Mandorlian system. I still don't fully understand it. It's their direct link with what they call "the Source" and with each other. At World Union, the only unity we have is forced on us through satellite coders that trace all our actions and translate all our human thoughts for AI. But we have no control over that.

Liainsee2 and Aco-rately r not rare

its just they have those gifs we all have, but they worked em. We can all dreamswim if we just practice n do tha work. This we know. But there r steps 2 get there. We know we need sun, n we can all get 2 that, even in WU. It just takes planning n effort to have it touch us bare. That activates tha melanin.

So why they not more islands like Ma-land, if most of tha humans on Earth have melanin? Friend, theres more than that needed 2 b a dreamswimma. And we dont know how many other islands there r. We du know that a dreamswimma has to b completely immersed in love 4 tha multiverse. And how many folks in WU have that, when that WU virus has sickened us 4 centuries with moneydoom, egoes n white control? Theres hardly any melanated humans 2 b found that r completely free of tha WU virus. Seen? They so sick they dont even know that all humans got melanin. They think just us brown ones do. Ha! Why u think tha core of all eyes, even cats n birds n fish is black? Thats tha center of it all. Tha porthole is in tha eyes. But its very important cause during mindwrap at 3am, we know tha moon's faint light is more easily absorbed when that melanin is activated. Its only n that bluelight that tha blueseeds r traceable. But u got 2 b able 2 open up your own porthole 2 yur own melanin. Seen? But even that melanin iz not enuf still without tha love. Tha love iz critical. That Dorla n Mon. Thats what they got. They got tha love.

Mandorlians, Ulysses Jenkins and Jeni Presnall, 2013.

THE DOLPHINS AND SWANS RETURN TO VENICE

Mandorla Awakening II: Emerging Worlds began with the question, "What would an advanced egalitarian society that is in harmony with nature be like?" The project will never really be done, and I recognize that my creative work is still crawling in the infant stages of responding to this question. It was my dream to share futuristic visions that open windows to other worlds, to inspire creativity in everything from greener architecture to new gestures of care between people. The *MA* projects have been rooted in my imagination of a technologically sophisticated, Earth-centered society, but these manifestations within the project have barely touched the surface. As a composer, it's fun to approach my work as a scientist experimenting with various ways to manifest a positive futuristic vision. But I also realize the limitations of my own imagination. I look forward to further experimentation and collaboration with others: talks, concerts,

Nicole Mitchell Gantt

and multi-arts projects. To see an increase of full-scale collaboration between artists and architects, inventors, and scientists from many fields with the intent of designing a more equitable, eco-sustainable world would be amazing.

With her "emotion picture" *Dirty Computer*, Janelle Monáe, the Afrofuturist storyteller, filmmaker, actress, composer, and vocalist, offers a vision of utopia where young people of all nationalities have the freedom to experience joy through dancing and togetherness, and where queer love is centralized. Monáe contrasts her imagined place of freedom with images of an oppressive society that unsuccessfully attempts to use technology to erase memories of hope, joy, and rebelliousness from the minds of its Black youth.

The challenge we all face to updating our humanity and dissolving the fallacies of systematic white hegemony is that we have to dive into the depths of western thought to do it. And we cannot immerse ourselves in the water without drinking it in. We are the poison we try to heal ourselves from. What are our blind spots?

We've been told that technology is key to human advancement. The mythology of technology tells us that new inventions and scientific discoveries will improve the human condition. My husband Calvin loves to tell the story of how, when we were in Mali, we enjoyed the fact that villagers were living old-school—entertaining each other by sharing stories and keeping company with one another. There was a rhythm to the day. At sunrise, the rooster crowed, and then immediately all the other animals joined in—moo, baa, and heehaw—to call for their breakfast. All that commotion was the rise and shine for folks to start their day. But one day, the rooster started crowing at 3 a.m., triggering the choir of animals, and everyone jumped up to start the day. Only then, in the dark, did they realize that someone forgot to turn off their cell phone before bed; its ring had stirred the rooster and thrown the whole day off.

Those of us connected to the digital network (the Ooloi tentacles) are so seduced by technology that we jump on each new update, gobbling up cell phones, computers, tablets, and social media accounts like candy. But the advancements in digital technology are not available to everyone, and they don't guarantee improved quality of life. In 2016, only 47% of the world's population used the internet.[60] Weren't we promised that computers would spare us from menial

---

60   Adam Taylor, "47 percent of the world's population now use the internet, study says," *The Washington Post*, November 22, 2016, https://www.washingtonpost.com/news/worldviews/wp/2016/11/22/47-percent-of-the-worlds-population-now-use-the-internet-users-study-says/.

labor? (Nope.) Or that cell phones, email, and online chat would ensure more efficient communication? (Didn't happen.) They say that robocars will minimize traffic accidents. (I doubt it.) Yet I am as addicted as anyone to my cell phone and wi-fi. Those of us who own phones and cars and fly in airplanes complain about racism, sexism, and homophobia, but our own habits and choices contribute to the suffering of others due to oil-infested waters, depleted soil, and war. A machine mouth chews through trees, Earth, and people to make money, but at some point, the jewels of nature will run out.

We have hit a wall.

I think it's now.

But despite all this talk, we won't abandon technology altogether. We love it too much!

The problem of technology is not the fault of the technology itself. The problem is that technology is being used as a tool for the purpose of greed (GDP) rather than human well-being.

Can we first accept that technology in itself will not bring about human "advancement"? That more money is not the key to progress? That change will not happen magically without some effort of collective intent and a lot of work? There's nowhere to hide in ignorance anymore, and we can't click our heels three times, snap our fingers, and expect our problems to go away.

We keep on doing the same thing, over and over and over again...

In April 2020, in the midst of stress and lockdown, some of us wanted to believe that dolphins and swans had returned to Venice, Italy. It was a breathtaking story of human imagination. People around the world shared images on Facebook images of dolphins and swans swimming happily in the empty waters surrounding Venice. These were hopeful dreams of nature healing in response to our forced shutdown of normal activities. Many thought that perhaps the Earth really can heal from our stupid destructive actions. In truth, there were no dolphins, but the pandemic did have one unexpected positive outcome: it temporarily slowed the seemingly unstoppable pollution of our environment by industrialized society.

The pandemic was a loud call for change. I would have hoped that a pandemic threatening all human life and the world economy and creating a crisis in unemployment, food scarcity, education, housing insecurity, and increased domestic and child abuse would rally people of all backgrounds in a collective fight for survival. If there was ever any question that racism compromised efforts toward real human progress, 2020 resolved it. But rather than bring us together to solve a global human issue, the virus spread more fear and mistrust. It did nothing to bridge the racial gap. Anti-Black violence in the US continued unabated, while existing disparities were exacerbated, as shown in disproportionate death rates. In February 2020, Ahmaud Arbery was chased down and assassinated while jogging. In March, Breonna Taylor was gunned down in her apartment. In May, George Floyd was choked to death in public. People possessed by the myth of white hegemony continued to violently and unjustly kill any Black or Brown person they could get their hands on. Why?

Systematic racism is the rotten core of what humanity needs to change for its survival.

A SCREAM

An alarm has been sounding.
There was a pic/nic

full of gaping onlookers who
enjoyed the twisted spectacle

with sandwiches and lemonade.
"Strange fruit" was a cook/out.

Then, they wore hoods
to hide their faces.
Icy teeth in sunshine, burning houses in the dark.

An alarm has been sounding.

The trees remember
bloodthirsty mouths
and Christian crosses that
scorched countless nights.
But the law.

Murder mobs illegal

So, faces hid to mask the joy of killing.

Ida Bell Wells
disrobed hate

made naked by her media.
Billie Holiday strung a strange song
shamed hard hearts with music.
Mamie Elizabeth
lifted Emmett's veil
An alarm is sounding.
Savage truth is seen

They hid their hoods and shamed uniforms.
Hands, knees and
angry mouths

mar whiteness

Nicole Mitchell Gantt

with thirst for black Death
Hoods hidden
kill with badges
An alarm is sounding.

Swallow blood with your black

guns and black night/sticks.
    with the heat of hate

Black is indestructible.
If you are shamed, move with us.

To make atonement, move with us.

We will disrobe with our pen
We will disrobe with our lyrics and cosmic music.
We will hold our cameras to unveil the savage truth
We will call, stand and protest
But it is you, the shamed that must end the thirst.

We re-mem

wa
whe
can
across the
towards

Nicole Mitchell Gantt

244

per another
of being,
e we
reach
universe
our Source.

("Staircase Struggle," *Mandorla Awakening*, 2015.)

The Mandorla Letters

Entry 7.

I'm scared. It seems that since we arrived, the mindwrap has become agitated from our fears.

This threatens to murk up the vision of collective purpose the Mandorlians communicate through the mindlake each day. Ma-land can become unstable just from our thoughts! Many Mandorlians feel strongly that it would be best for us to leave as soon as possible. We've already upset the natural balance as visitors of Mandorla, although we are at great risk if we go back to WU during this Egoes War. Yet mindwrap has told the Mandorlians that we are not completely foreign. Mon has seen the mindlake. We arrived here through our love. But although we've been introduced to beginning concepts of meditation, we might not be ready or have the talents to participate in mindwrap sessions. Everyone has to participate in mindwrap to stay here, to continue the manifestation of the island. To continue this beautiful way of life. I think we should go back to WU, but now Mon likes it here. I'm not sure what to do.

The Mandorla Letters

UNDOING RACE FOR A MORE COLLAB- ORATIVE GAME

In summer 2020, I saw on Facebook a video of a group of young people getting ready to run a race. At the starting line, the coach asked for only those with two parents to take two steps forward, then only those who didn't have to help their parents with the bills to take two steps forward, then only those who went to private school to take two steps forward, then only those who were never hungry to take two steps forward, and so on. After finishing his prompts, the coach had those who had taken steps forward turn around and look at the people behind them. All the people at the very back were Black and Brown, and all the people at the very front were white. He told these young people that their position relative to others had absolutely nothing to do with any individual effort they made, but rather it was due to their privilege (or lack of it) alone. If the playing field were fair, he said, then some of the Black and Brown youth could win the race no problem because of their

Nicole Mitchell Gantt

abilities. But rather than align them all back to equal footing, he told them they had to start the race where they stood. He said, "Ready, set, go! Go ahead and run your race!"

The Civil Rights Movement, led by Black people in the US, was a national struggle for everyone to have a more even playing field—to make the race of life in American society more equitable for all humans. Those efforts have been mostly dismantled because of society's infatuation with the western thought-agreement bent on power and hegemony. So I ask, like Morpheus in *The Matrix*, "And you think that's air you're breathing now?" Rather than re-engaging work to even the playing field, shouldn't we aim to change the game entirely? Why are we running a race that only a few are allowed to win? Let's make a new game with new rules that secure true collaboration where everyone can win.

If we reshape the parameters by which we measure progress to prioritize universal human well-being in harmony with the planet, technology can help us to achieve our goal. Technology is a great tool, if utilized with holistic, humane intent. But a real step forward would be a willingness to untangle ourselves from this idea of status and money and being first, and to utilize our competitive spirit toward motivating humaneness. We have a lot of work ahead of us, for sure, but my intuition says we can move forward if we learn to respect the experience of each individual, culture, and community and use this collective wisdom toward achieving Oneness in humanity.

The universe is sending this message to us, and many are hearing it:

It is possible to enter a transformation of human consciousness toward healing ourselves, respecting the Earth, establishing balance, and reawakening spirituality.

In *Cruising Utopia*, José Esteban Muñoz refers to our need to reach for the *not-yet*. We, as humans, are in-process; or as Sylvia Wynter says, "being human is a praxis." The horizon holds promise, and through our imaginations, we can manifest positive visions in our now and tomorrow.

Hey Deondra,

Thanks for the notes on Banneker. I always wanted to learn more about him but never made the time.

Hey…just know you can always come here and stay with us on the farm if you need to. We have plenty of space and Tadique's vegetables are coming up so HUGE. That's what's keeping us sane. I know everything is f**d up right now and I don't expect you to write back, but I have to say, I am encouraged to see all those young white people protesting with us. In the end, they are going to have to be the ones that stop this. Not for us, but for themselves. They must be so ashamed to be white right now. Those crazy evil people make them look bad. People just casually, *casually* killing People of Color because they say they felt threatened? What does that say about their humanity? Don't get me started. Talk about SAVAGE! That's what savage looks like to me, for real. They treat dogs better. They LOVE their pets. It's just so simple. Can you love us like you love your relatives? Our relatives come in all shades and shapes as Black folk. But these folks just can't seem to *see* us. Or maybe it means they hate themselves the way they hate us.

On your earlier note, I totally get it that you want to move to Ghana. Especially now. George Floyd—that was the last straw. I totally feel you. Everything feels like it's going to hell. I've always wanted to go there and now that they officially are welcoming African Americans and opening it up for us, that's a beautiful opportunity. It's just that our whole family is HERE and you know I've got a big family. And sh*t, we built this motherf**kr and we from here too. We Black Indians.

I heard that your Auntie got sick. I'm so sorry. I know this is a hard time for you. I'm glad your son didn't get mixed up with the National Guard at the protest. Please be safe. I was thinking about

Sweet Honey in the Rock. Such a beautiful vocal group. Remember that song that goes:

Until the killing of Black men, Black mother's sons,
is as important as the killing of white men, white mother's sons,
WE WHO BELIEVE IN FREEDOM SHALL NOT REST.

Hey, BTW, on a *lighter* note, we were just talking about Octavia's *Parables*, right? Well, Toshi Reagon and adrienne maree brown started a podcast called *Octavia's Parables* this month! Remember Toshi Reagon—Bernice Johnson Reagon's daughter who made the opera about *Parable of the Sower*? They are gonna start with *Parable of the Sower*, breaking it down chapter by chapter. That's gonna be dope.

BTW, Octavia Butler's birthday was a few days ago.

Peace, Love and Light for your Fam,
Reesy
Xx

THE SHINY DIVIDER (PART 2)

Red..........lava.........!
burns...........with.....sweat.........!

the......earth....!
is.....melting.......!

the land is shaking!
but we keep on walking that way!

the nuclear plants are leaking!
but we keep on walking that way!

the oceans are filled with plastic bags!
the fish are choking!

but we keep on walking that way!
blood is spilling!

but we keep on walking that way!
our blood is spilling in Baltimore, Ferguson, and Nepal!

but it doesn't seem to bother us at all!
we keep on walking that way!

whoa oo oo!
let's turn around!

whoa oo oo!
there's a cliff around the corner!

whoa oo oo!
I want to pick up my blade!
there's got to be a better way!

whoa oo oo!
let's go another way!

we can come together now!

Blood ...... is........spilling........!
we.....keep..............on...........!
Blood ...... is........spilling........!
we.....keep..............on...........!

Nicole Mitchell Gantt

252

illing!

but we

walking

ay.

eep   on

March 22–2100

Liansee2, Check these out. I found these on a memory bit at tha shores. They were a bit scrambled. But I was able 2 open em on grandmamas computa n recalibraided tha lingo 4 us. Wow. Some of it was writn by old WU artises from be4. N some by our chilren. Somthin else, ya no? Writtn be4 WU corruptd 2 total chaos from egoes wars. Artises was tryna to find others. Was makn some new collective 2 rebuild/rethink? Seen? It shows some a em was on tha verge of dreamswimmn before egoes wars! Dreamswimmn just ba4 dissolution! Artises was making music 2. They not find blueseed. Traced our codes. They made a project for Ma-land! Somehow they talk of our Ephemera Island, Ma-land! They perhaps seen shadow mindlake n saw us here? Proves they potential. Ah, bless. There might b more back then there 2 help us reassemble! Lets check in tha mindwrap 4 them 2nite.

fondly, Acorately.

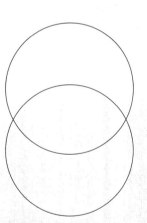